Confessions
of an
Archery Mom

Praise for
Confessions of an Archery Mom

"What a wonderfully written book! At times I laughed, at times I cried, sometimes both. This book is for all parents and coaches who have helped their child navigate the special and sometimes crazy world of youth sports. It's also the book for those who have just embarked upon that thrilling, fulfilling and at times wacky ride!"

Helen Sahi
Archery Coach, Hockey Coach,
Mother of Jr. World Champion Alex Sahi

"Any parent who coaches their own children will enjoy Lorretta's witty and wry stories about how she took her sons from novices to state and national champions and Olympic Trials participants in archery. Her humerous views make this book an enjoyable read for everyone. It also explains all the things a coach and parent needs to know to help their children compete successfully in archery or any other sport."

Catherine Gannon
CEO of C.E. Zurn & Associates

"If you want to understand how passion for a sport can dictate and rule your life, understand the work it takes to raise or become a champion and how sharing such a passion within your family can enrich your family life, read *Confessions of an Archery Mom*.

Ed Eliason
Archery Olympian

"Reading this book gave ne a very strong sense of *deja vu*. The settings and names were different but the stories paralleled many of my family's experiences in our archery journey. The irony is that the most important lessons we learned *through* archery had nothing to do *with* archery.

As I read *Confessions of an Archery Mom* I was reminded of John Lennon's line from has song *Beautiful Boy*: "Life is what happens to you when you are busy making other plans." That is what archery has been for hundreds of families like ours around the U.S. and the world.

One of my favorite descriptions of a parent's or a coach's role is as a catalyst: someone who sparks activity where previously there was none or gets groups to interact with one another. An other part of being a catalyst is that you are not one of the raw materials, nor are you the final product, but without the catalyst, there is no transformation. Lorretta's role as an Archery Mom perfectly illustrates that role as a catalyst. I loved every word!

Tom Barker
Archery Coach and Archery Dad

Confessions of an Archery Mom

by Lorretta Sinclair

WATCHING ARROWS FLY, LLC

Lorretta Sinclair

Library of Congress Cataloging-in Publication Data

Confessions of an Archery Mom / Lorretta Sinclair.
  p. cm
  ISBN 978-0-9848860-0-5 (softcover)
  1. Archery. 2. Memoir. I Lorretta Sinclair

ISBN: 978-0-9848860-0-5

The web addresses cited in this text were current as of August 2011, unless otherwise noted.

Writer: Lorretta Sinclair; **Copy Editor**: Steve Ruis; **Proofreader**: Claudia Stevenson; **Cover Designer**: Steve Ruis; ; **Book Designer**: Steve Ruis; **Photographers** (cover and interior): Lorretta Sinclair unless otherwise noted

Printed in the United States of America 10 9 8 7 6 5 4 3 2

Watching Arrows Fly
3712 North Broadway, #285
Chicago, IL 60613
312.505.9770
www.watchingarrowsfly.com

Dedication

For Clarke, Dakota, and Barrett

Our adventures have given me gray hair, sleepless nights, anxiety . . . and I wouldn't have missed them for the world.

Our archery experience is inspired by great people who took the time to work with not only the boys, but with Bob and I; to teach us, if nothing else, to be present. It took a team to get us to where we are and it will continue to take a team, comprised of the people we trust most, to continue the journey. The lessons we've learned along the way and the people we've met whose wisdom and knowledge we have received matters greatly to me.

I always told my boys when they were little that "in your lifetime you will only ever have a handful of people you can truly count on." And the one unequivocal thing they could always count on is that the five of us stand together. We are fortunate, that we also have so many archery friends who stand with us. That is a constant in our lives and as an archery mom and coach that never changed.

And while some would say that Clarke is not here, I say he's always here, he's always with us, and the most important thing we learned in archery is the very thing I taught them as little boys before we ever bought a bow, or let go of an arrow – we five stand together.

I want to thank my husband, affectionately dubbed "Bobert" by my sons. He has deftly ridden the waves of my Archery Mom days. He's watched our boys in their ups and their downs. He's become an Equipment Geek to support their archery habits and he's worked to pay the bills for them. He's supported my College Archery efforts, including when College Archery was literally a line item in our family budget just to get some basics done for the program. And he's the joy in my heart not only on good days, but more importantly, on the days that are the darkest.

Table of Contents

Forward		*xi*
Introduction		*xii*
1	Archery Mom: How'd I Get This Gig Anyway?	1
2	You Know You're an Archery Mom When . . .	9
3	Archery and Real Estate–Getting the Priorities Right	15
4	Wind Practice	23
5	What's a Little Heat When You are Having Fun?	29
6	Learning to Use a Bow Sight	35
7	Life Lessons in Archery	41
8	Tournament Time!	47
9	True Grit	53
10	Traveling with Shade	59
11	An Archery Mom's Guide to House Cleaning	67
12	The Money Pit	73
13	Be Humble . . .	79
14	Telling on Mom	85
15	The Art of Staying Focused When Things Go Terribly Wrong	91
16	Bow Tuning–Whew, Who Knew?	95
17	It's a Team Effort	103
18	The Mom Card	111
19	Dislocated in the Dominican Republic	117
20	Finding the F-U-N in Archery Again	129
21	Aged Out (The Boys Grow Up)	139
22	Random Things I Have Learned as an Archery Mom	145
	About the Author	*153*
	Archery Terminology for the Unfamiliar	*159*

Lorretta Sinclair

Foreword

by Ed Eliason

Since early childhood, I have been obsessed with the physics and mechanics of how an arrow flies. To describe the satisfaction gained from the disciplined focus of archery is difficult. There is just something about a well-loosed arrow flying through the air and hitting your target with a congratulatory thwack that makes me . . . happy. Lorretta captures this concept, this feeling familiar to all archers, regardless of ability:

> . . . *Just shooting because the feel of cleanly loosing an arrow is something that few people actually get to do in the world and knowing that feeling, that essence of the arrow flying 200 feet per second towards a piece of paper and landing in the 10 ring, that feeling of success, for the intrinsic value of that, that's what archery [is about].* . . .

If you want to understand how passion for a sport can dictate and rule your life; the work it takes to raise or become a champion and how sharing such a passion within your family can enrich your family life, read *Confessions of an Archery Mom*. Oh, it will also educate you on the time, money, travel, money, frustrations, money, pain, money, disciplined hard(!) work, and . . . oh, did I mention money? . . . that an archery addiction will cost you, as well as the total satisfaction and camaraderie it can provide.

Anyone who has been involved in elite sports, either as a participant, parent, or coach, knows that the sport permeates your life in very unexpected ways. In this book, Archery Mom Lorretta Sinclair explains (or should I say warns about) the unavoidable change of your "normal" perspective: the house-buying concerns of an archery-addicted family, the purposeful loss of sanity necessary to "live" archery (which prevents an assuredly inadvertent fall into madness), flying with archery equipment (don't forget the shade), housecleaning around archers, coaching children with different ways of learning and executing, archery "life" lessons, and understanding that "it costs extra." Most importantly, what the Sinclairs learned and Lorretta shares, is that if your sense of self gets lost in the fray of competition, remember what is intrinsically important to you, why you became an Archer (or Archery Family) in the first place, re-assess your goals, and get the F-U-N back in the game.

While *Confessions of an Archery Mom* is told with a good dose of humor, it also portrays deep life lessons of sportsmanship, diligence, success, failure, and patience. During their archery adventures, the Sinclair family suffered a devastating loss, at which time they must have felt lost. But, ever the Archery Mom, Lorretta shows us how archery—and their extended archery family—helped them at first survive, then heal, then move forward.

A Confession —err, umm— Introduction

My adventure as an Archery Mom started with a birthday present consisting of one recurve bow and an archery lesson and ended up taking us on adventures we would have never imagined.

The first time my sons actually shot a bow was with a little Walmart plastic thing as part of their Cub Scout experience in our backyard in Inyokern, CA when our boys were 9, 6, and 3. I really thought nothing more about it other than they earned their Cub Scout achievement award as outlined in the Cub Scout handbook.

Who would have guessed that several years later, as our son Clarke was about to turn 13, my husband Bob would suggest getting him a bow for his birthday and we would embark on an unexpected adventure. But, that's exactly what happened. The series of events that led us into the sport of archery, also led us to meet a number of amazing people. Our lack of experience and knowledge in archery makes us laugh as we look back to the first experience purchasing a bow and then falling in love with a sport that we knew nothing about. We had no dreams, no aspirations; heck we didn't even know archery was a competitive sport, much less an Olympic sport. And that's not why we wanted to get Clarke a bow in the first place. We simply wanted something unique for him to do and we knew that he seemed to enjoy that one brief experience when he was six years old.

As a homeschooling family we had not involved our sons in competitive sports, but rather enjoyed camping, hiking, raising pure-bred chickens, and pursuing family togetherness by hanging out with one another. It turned out that archery was the perfect sport for our family, for having fun, and for pursuing the eventual lofty goals of our three sons to make World Teams and possibly go to the Olympics some day. But one thing we are known for and good at is giving 100% when we decide to do something.

Archery gave our family a focus and it also gave my sons, Dakota, Clarke, and Barrett the opportunity to participate in a sport that was all about each one's goals, successes, failures, and abilities. You either hit the 10 or you didn't. Nobody else controlled that. (Well, there were the times they tried to distract each other at full draw to make one mess up; but we're not counting brotherly love here.) Together we embarked on a journey that has been fun, sad, difficult, heartbreaking, full of joy and laughter . . . and expensive. But we were together, learning all the time and that was worth every dime (well, pretty much every dime).

Our journey started in Salt Lake City, Utah where we first bought the boys' equipment and joined the Utah Hot Shots at Salt Lake Archery. Owner Larry Smith's ability to teach archery is amazing. Larry was their instructor and sometimes he scared the Hell out of me when he wasn't in a good mood, but he always had a special sparkle when it came to teaching archery to kids. His affinity for Barrett, who started at the age of 10 and was overshadowed in the beginning by his big brothers, developed into a relationship that even now as Barrett turns 20 is a strong bond between them that will be there forever. Clarke loved to give Larry a hard time. He had, at one point, dubbed him Scary Larry—in jest—just to see what his reaction would be. (Larry laughed.) Larry is now part of our family and has shared in our biggest joys and our deepest sorrows.

Since we weren't involved in bowhunting, like the vast majority of archers in Utah, we didn't know that choosing to shoot recurve equipment would mean that we would be joining a very small group of target archers. I'm not even sure we knew there was such a thing as bowhunting. But one day we heard there was an archery range at the Hunter's Education Center so we checked that out and sure enough, Paradise, an amazing indoor archery range. Northern Utah is cold pretty much eight months of the year (well, for a native Californian it's cold that many months, even if my Utah friends say I'm exaggerating).

At the Hunter Education Center, we were introduced to Herb and Luann Mays, their son Lynn, and Lynn's son Cody, as well as Mike and Claudia Beeny, their daughter Jennifer, and grandchildren Marae, Riley, and Havila. They were all part of the Cache Archers, including Pat Madison, headquartered at the Hunter Ed Center. The boys joined the archery league and since there weren't many kids, they shot with the adults . . . who were all compound archers. Not a recurve bow in sight and, in fact, people would come in and ask, "What is that thing?" as if they'd never seen one, but mostly they teased the boys mercilessly because their mom wouldn't let their archery friends "handicap" them when they shot against the adult compound archers. Our boys were working hard to be good and I was so naive that I didn't realize the disadvantage faced by recurve bow archers when shooting against compound bows. I wouldn't budge. "No handicaps. Shoot it straight up. Get good enough and you'll beat them."

In mid 2003, Clarke and Dakota determined they wanted to try out for the Junior World Archery Team. The trials were being hosted in Tooele, Utah, about 45 minutes away from Salt Lake City. This was a daunting challenge. They'd taken their first lesson barely a year before. They'd only been competing for seven or eight months and now they were telling us they wanted to make a World Team. Okay, here we go. . . .

How do you train to make a world team when you live in a place that starts snowing in October, temperatures dip to -30° F, and you have five feet of snow on the ground. And even though you have an indoor range, it's only 18 meters and you need to be good at 70 meters? We had no clue, so we started asking questions, and sure enough Herb came through. He knew a guy who knew a guy who owned a pallet company. Four nights a week, we were able to use the giant warehouse with pallets stacked 10 feet high and a narrow pathway left for us to set up and shoot. It was cold in the warehouse but nothing like the temperatures outside. So we practiced at night in the warehouse and on the weekends we went to the Hunters Ed Center or to lessons in Salt Lake. As soon as it looked remotely like we could get them outside, we set up the matts on our own FITA range. Dressed in multiple layers of clothes, they stood in three feet of snow, freezing rain, hail, and whatever else came at them and shot. And to our surprise, when we asked the Cache Archers to help us get them ready by shooting against the boys, they showed up.

Watching the cars coming down our long driveway, people pulling out bows, and coolers and chairs (and those warmer days when Jennifer brought us all Jamba Juices!), knowing it was freezing cold but also knowing Dakota and Clarke were determined to make the team, we knew that archery wasn't just a sport. Archery is a family.

And the boys started beating their compound friends—without a handicap! And we barbecued at the mid-point of the FITA rounds, just like all good archery families.

Clarke made the Jr. World Team on June 3rd of 2004, barely two years from his first lesson with Larry. Dakota placed 10th; he was sorely disappointed but determined then and there that he would make a World Team and he did two years later, travelling to Slovakia on the World University Team. Dakota subsequently made three more World Teams. Barrett had changed from shooting left-handed to right- handed and struggled sometimes to keep up, but the smile on his face the day he won the 2007 World Target Championships in the Cadet Division in Colorado showed us all what determination means.

Now that we knew there were differences between compound bows and recurve bows, and now that we knew we had not invented outdoor shooting, we landed in the expert hands of Mike Gerard and Ed Eliason. Mike was a world record holder at the age of 13. Mike also shoots recurve *and* compound bows *and* is very good at both. And I hesitate to say, "more importantly" but I'm going to, more importantly Mike is an archery geek! And a geek is what we needed! Because geeks have knowledge and Mike is an encyclopedia. Ed, is not only an encyclopedia but he is a master of mental games, including playing them on young archers when they aren't paying attention! Just ask Ed about setting off clickers early to see how someone will react and you'll get the broad smile of, "Well that's fun!" Between Mike and Ed, the Sinclair family learned more about archery in a year than we would have in a lifetime without knowing them.

When the boys started competing I understood that I needed to learn as much as I could about the world of competitive archery. So, I took coaching certification courses, and we read whatever we could find on the internet. We purchased the few books on the subject that were in print and everyone devoured them. And we started travelling, usually me with the boys so Bob could earn the money to support our new habit. I "confess" in "The Mom Card" and "Finding the F-U-N in Archery Again" chapters that I get frustrated and exasperated. Life is full of frustrations and I had to learn to find a balance that often was (and still is) a struggle.

As I explain in "Bow Tuning—Whew, Who Knew" and "The Money Pit," we learned early on that archery can be an expensive sport. It is not a sport that recurve archers make a living at (for the most part) in the United States. As a one-income family, it has always been a struggle to fund all of the equipment and travel expenses. And we had to do it times three! If one boy needed a new bow sight, amazingly the other two needed one also. If someone was ready to get a different riser, it was tough to tell the other two that they had to wait. And the little things —those doggone *Spin Wings* and such—pound for pound cost more than prime beef. They should be gold plated, but we figured out a way to buy them because, well, in the words of Clarke, "I need them." The expense of travelling with three boys put financial pressure on the family. But the boys had done everything we'd asked as far as practicing, learning about equipment, and preparing to compete, so we did what all archery families do—we made it happen. I think I had travelled by plane maybe two or three times before archery. Now, I've travelled all over the country, and outside the country, as well as learned to manage three boys, bowcases, a pop-up shade, and all of the ins and outs of tournament travel. It wasn't easy, and many times it wasn't fun. But it was always an adventure.

Archery also became our safety net when tragedy struck in September 2004. Barely six weeks after Clarke came home from the Jr. World Championships in Lilleshall, England, our family lost him at the age of 15 years and 7 months. The day before the accident, Clarke and Barrett were outside practicing. Clarke had asked if he could help coach Barrett and what a great opportunity that was for each of them. Clarke and Barrett had a great relationship, Clarke often laying on the floor of their bedroom, bored silly, but watching Barrett play Legos just to keep him company. That day, Clarke was working with Barrett on his release. Mike Gerard had once commented that Clarke had "one of the cleanest releases I've ever seen." And indeed, it was having a beautiful release that Clarke wanted to teach to his brother. I sat out on the porch watching them and as they walked down to gather arrows, Clarke had his arm wrapped around his little brother's shoulders and was literally beaming as he yelled up to me, "Hey mom! He shot a 56! at 50m!" and then he rubbed Barrett's head and said loud enough that I could hear it, "You're going to be better than me someday! I'll make sure of that!"

That same afternoon, Clarke finished his own practice with his dad watching him. I glanced out the windows as they walked back and forth while Clarke talked about trying to make the Jr. World Indoor Team a few months later. He had spent the night putting a spread-sheet together of the scores of the top archers which he printed out and handed to me, "Here're the scores I need to beat," he said. As I glanced at the piece of paper I laughed so hard, "But Clarke, you are going to try out as a Cadet, why do you have the scores of Butch Johnson, Vic Wunderle, and Staten Holmes on here?" In true Clarke fashion, he replied, "Because Mom, I'm not just training to beat the cadets, I'm training to be the best in the world, so I'm going to beat those scores."

I lost my son the next morning in a terrible accident and he died in my arms as I told him over and over how lucky I was that he was my son. Life will never be the same. Clarke was the cog in our wheel. He was the mid-dle man. He was the best friend to each of his brothers. He was my buddy, and to his Dad, whom he had nick-named "Bobert," he was an amazing young man whom Bob admired for his integrity. You never get over losing your child; you just find ways to help cover that hole in your heart. For us, archery took on a different meaning. It was all we could figure out to do to distract ourselves.

We poured our hearts and souls into archery. We started the Clarke Sinclair Memorial Archery Scholarship (*www.clarkesinclair.org*) in honor of Clarke. We wanted to keep Clarke's love of archery alive by helping other youth and college archers when they made World Teams by pro-viding small scholarships. Dakota and Barrett kept com-peting and I kept up as the chauffeur, travel agent and Archery Mom. I started a Junior Olympic Archery Development Program with Lynn and Herb Mays for kids in Cache Valley, and Bob and I continued to learn all that we could to help Dakota and Barrett succeed.

The boys eventually outgrew the youth program. As college students both Dakota and Barrett are members of the US Collegiate Archery Association (USCA). As the Executive Director of USCA, I "expanded" from being an archery mom to my sons, to now watch over more than 500 college students learn and participate in this fabulous sport.

I hope the stories in this book educate, or amuse, or even inspire you Archery Moms and Dads out there.

Lorretta Sinclair
November 2011

Lorretta Sinclair

◎1◎

How'd I Get This Archery Mom Gig Anyway?

Date   1 April 2002
Time   5 PM
Place   Salt Lake Archery, Salt Lake City, UT
Event   Clarke's 13th birthday, His 1st Archery Lesson,
        and Beginner's Night
Reason We thought "He'd like it."

Really, this was the impetus for my becoming an Archery Mom.

Yeah, I actually know the exact date when I started on the path to becoming an Archery Mom. While some people spend their kid's formative years going to lessons, participating in a JOAD (Junior Olympic Archery Development) program, and then growing into competing, well, that's not my story. Like many things in my life, things happen while I am not looking and I find myself in an adventure that I did not plan, did not anticipate, and would not have even thought about. Life happens and, in this case, stumbling into archery has worked out . . . I think.

Becoming an Archery Mom was a rather speedy process, feeling later like I'd been caught up in a whirlwind, my feet not touching the ground as my sons worked their way into the USA Archery national rankings. Some of it had, I am sure, to do with the fact that Salt Lake Archery, owned by Larry and Randi Smith, is a hub for archery and home to many top-ranked U.S. archers, as well as being a site for national competitive events. We fell into archery without realizing what was about to hit us. We knew nothing. And I'm not kidding. Nothing!

My husband Bob and I stood in Salt Lake Archery in March 2002, trying to determine what to buy Clarke for his birthday. The seemingly gruff man in the wheelchair, totally exasperated by our ignorance, finally told us it would be best if we brought our son in to choose his own bow. I wanted the present to be a surprise, but in light of our dilemma, we agreed. The day of his birthday, we announced we were going to take an archery lesson and Clarke would get to pick out a bow. Later, at the shop, Clarke was given an option between compound and recurve bows (we didn't know the names then, I learned them later). He chose the "long curvy one" because "I like its shape" (the recurve bow) over the "one with wheels" (the compound bow). The only indication that we were making a good decision, or at least one that someone agreed with, was when Larry Smith looked at Clarke and happily said, "Good choice! Now let's get some arrows." He wasn't nearly as annoyed with Clarke about not knowing anything as he was with us, the parents, who asked all kinds of seemingly obvious questions.

After getting him all set up with a *Bullseye* wood bow and Easton aluminum arrows, it was time to start his archery lessons. We sat in the parent's viewing section and watched as our three sons had a great time shooting "bows and arrows" for the first time. Within a month,

Larry had given little 10-year-old Barrett a bow and 16-year-old Dakota had purchased his own *Bullseye* bow from his savings. Larry's patience in teaching the boys to shoot was, and is, unsurpassed.

Within three months, Bob had found plans for an "archery target stand" and was busy pounding nails into 2x4s to build what the boys ended up calling "the popsicle stand." We didn't know there were actual commercially available outdoor target matts and stands to support them—we thought we were in the forefront of building a way to shoot outside! The completed target stand looked like a place to sit down and sell popsicles and lemonade, except we had straw bales on it as our backstop. When we finally did see real matts and outdoor stands, we laughed hard at our naiveté.

We started out making the three hour round trip from our home in Logan, Utah to Salt Lake City once a week for the boys' lessons. The boys loved it so much that by the time we were six months into it, we were going twice a week. At that point, Larry introduced us to his JOAD program and we signed up, now making the long drive three times a week. One night, Clarke and Dakota saw a flier about something called "The Great Pumpkin Shoot." I hadn't even entertained the idea of competitions at that point, we were just having fun learning to shoot. The three-times a week trips were fun and we liked watching the boys . . . but they had different ideas. Quizzing Larry about "The Great Pumpkin Shoot" tournament, he told them they could shoot in it if they wanted to. They had never participated in any kind of event like this before and were eager to try, so with only six months experience, they participated in their first archery tournament. That's the moment I became an Archery

Mom. The night of the tournament I sat and watched my sons perform under pressure, lights, and whistles, with me sick to my stomach whenever an arrow scored a 3, and elated in triumph when one managed its way to the yellow for a 9 or 10. Clarke finished third that tournament and said, "I'll be practicing more; third place is embarrassing!" while his brother Dakota, who also finished third in his age category, concurred.

From that point in time, my life has twisted and turned and morphed into something I never imagined. Some days I long for the playfulness of JOAD nights where life sometimes was no more serious than shooting at a string of balloons tacked to the matts. Sometimes, I marvel at how far the boys came in a short amount of time. And I always shake my head at how I became, without any knowledge or planning or my consent, an Archery Mom. But, our family is known for doing things one hundred percent, so with the seriousness of the boys' intentions to compete nationally, I became a certified USA Archery Coach, an equipment geek learning how to tune bows for elite competition, and the coach/manager for my sons. I had a lot of help from the Smiths, Coach Mike Gerard, and eventually a few others. We bought and read all of the books on the subject we could find and we spent hours and hours discussing archery, watching videos, and practicing. And then, in the company of Dakota and Clarke, I made my foray into traveling to tournaments and got the bumps and bruises that go along with it.

Our sons outgrew "the popsicle stand" shortly after they finished roofing it with their dad. We found out about "real" target matts and "real" target stands, purchasing several used ones and setting up a practice range on our six acres of land. This benefited the boys greatly as they were able to come in and out of the house for lunch and breaks and practice without having to drive anywhere, although our drives to Salt Lake City continued. We found ourselves totally enveloped in the world of archery.

Our first outdoor tournament was the 2003 JOAD Nationals, fourteen months from the time the boys took their first lesson. A lot of people don't realize that archery is an "open sport," allowing anyone with the entry fee for a tournament to participate. This allows even archers who know they aren't ready to get the experience of a national tournament under their belts. Dakota wasn't shooting enough draw weight to make the Junior age category distances, so with much hesitation he shot in the Archer division; determined that by 2004 he would be in the top of the Junior ranks. Clarke shot in the Cub age division (12-14 years), and as he later said in a television interview in 2004, "Finished an embarrassing 17th" and determined that he'd "Be at the top next year."

At the end of the 2004 season, as they both predicted, 15-year old Clarke was ranked 4th in the country and 24th in the world, while 18-year-old Dakota was ranked 8th in his division in the U.S. having finished 4th at the 2004 JOAD Nationals, quite a change from being in the Archer division the previous year. Even 12-year old Barrett was in the top 10 in his division. Clarke had made the Junior World Team and we (Clarke and I) traveled to England taking competition and travel to a whole new level as this was the first time either of us had traveled outside of the United States.

By the end of 2006, Dakota was a two-time All-American. He had shot his way onto his first international team and traveled to Slovakia, and had made it into the top four in the USA Archery ranking system. Barrett was moving along very well, spending eight months changing from shooting left-handed to shooting right-handed, and had begun traveling to tournaments outside of our state as well. Clarke forever shoots 10's along side his brothers, always with perfect form and the admirable qualities he brought to us. And I had fallen in love with college archery, taking my "Archery Mom" gig to being Publicist for the College Division and continuing to coach the boys.

Looking back over that year, I know other people saw what was happening. It would've been fair to warn me. I didn't know that my life was going to be transformed without having an inkling such a change was coming. I didn't know that I would travel the world in order for my sons to shoot archery. I wish someone would have told me that when archery gets in your veins, "normal" never applies to you again. The secret was kept well as we went from learning to shoot, to the boys wanting to compete, to deciding they wanted to be ranked nationally, and then finally to setting the goal of making future Olympic and

Clarke and his Jr. World Team teammates

World Teams. The day Clarke made the Junior World Team, Larry Smith and Mike Gerard (both of whom had worked with Clarke) sat beaming under our canopy in Tooele, Utah. They knew the secret. They knew we were hooked on archery. There should be a warning sign on all archery shops to help us moms. It should be a requirement when signing the parental consent and registration forms for archery competitions. There should be a legal warning requiring acknowledgement before we buy any archery equipment. It's only fair—it's only right to protect us from ourselves:

> **Warning!
> Archery is
> addictive.
> You are in
> danger of
> becoming an
> Archery Mom!**

You Know You're an Archery Mom When . . .

With the birth of Dakota in 1986, I gave up my large, heavy, and always full of junk purse and traded it in for a baby bag. That bag was always full of the usual accoutrements of babyhood: diapers, clean clothes, wipes . . . and I carried my wallet, brush, and sunglasses in there as well, figuring that since I didn't have much personal stuff, I didn't need a purse anymore. With three boys separated by three years each, it was a long time before I had to give up the baby bag, and it never did become the "junk collector" that my previously large purse had become over time.

But the day came ten years later, that we no longer needed the baby bag going everywhere with us. I put it aside and found myself carrying my few but now growing "necessity" items with me. This lead to purchasing a small purse as I was determined not to carry a large "junk" purse again.

Alas, two years into archery, I discovered I am a true Archery Mom. This occurred to me one day when I was looking through my small purse for change to pay a coffee bill at a bookstore. Let's see here, well, I have some

Beiter *In/Out* nocks in both black and white, but I see the clerk has no interest in them as payment. I keep digging for a few quarters, but no, I come up with some pin nocks for one of my son's ACE arrows. Oh, and then look, here's some red nocks to fit on those pins. Hmm, any quarters in there? The clerk seemed perplexed as I pulled strange things from my purse but kept his comments, if not his smirk, to himself. Finally, I find enough change to pay the bill and sit down to read a magazine and drink my coffee.

I need to make some notes, so I again look in the bag for a pen and some semblance of paper to scribble on. Dig, dig, dig. Well, I can't find a pen, but I do have a Sharpie marker that is used to initial arrows at tournaments. Not easy to write with, but it's a better option than the red paint pen that I also find in the bag. Now I need some paper. Dig, dig, Multi-tool? Nope, that's for adjusting sights and fixing finger tabs. No wonder the purse seemed heavy. Hey, look, there are two multi-tools; you know the kind, a Swiss Army knife style of tool kit in one. Oh yeah, that's from when we were setting the center shot on that Martin *Aurora*. Why do I have them? Why aren't they in the gear bag? I don't know, so I throw them back in the purse and keep looking for paper. Ah, here's something to write on . . . nope, can't use that. That's one of the boys score sheets from the latest tournament. I am supposed to input the scores into our database. Better not mess it up with notes. Keep digging! Okay, just dump the purse out; that might work.

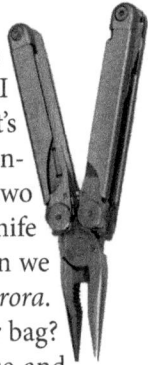

Slowly as I withdraw all the items from the bag, I find myself hoping to actually have time to make notes before I am to pick up my sons to go to archery practice. As I empty the bag, I am amused at what has become of my "little no-junk purse." I take out one of my son's extra finger tabs. I have it because I am supposed to cut a new face for it and thought that I would remember to do that if I stuck it in my purse. I have such a large assortment of nocks, I could probably fix any number of arrows at a tournament with little effort. What is this sticking to a market receipt? Oh, yuck, that darn *Fast Set* adhesive leaked again and is stuck to the receipts. Should make a note not to put that in my purse; it's too messy. I finally get to the bottom of the bag to find the most telling items of all. The heaviest things have to come out last since they are at the very bottom.

Now, embarrassingly, all of the contents are spread out on the table in the coffee shop, even six ACE break-off arrow points. Well, you never know when you might need them. They could come in handy while shopping for umm, err, I don't know. There must be some other use for them! Golf tees, for putting up target faces, maybe. Don't you always have some handy? Egad! This is terrible. I am an archery junkie! No, no, . . . I am an *Archery Mom*. Only a dedicated Archery Mom would have such things in her purse, so when one kid needs his nocks, you can easily pull them out and hand them over. Hey, you need a small screwdriver? Which type? I've got a little flathead screwdriver and a Phillips screwdriver, so I can take care of the two most common types of screws. What do you mean you can't find your primary finger tab? Where's your back up? Oh, in my purse? I was supposed to make a new face for it, I remember now. Heck, I even have an extra divider and an extra ledge for this tab because I saw them

laying on the table and thought we might need to replace worn parts. Finally, I realize I should just go ask someone for a piece of paper. It would've been a lot easier than scrounging through this mess.

Slowly, I begin reassembling the little purse. I place things back in the small pockets, ensuring the nocks are in one area, then in go the Sharpies, golf tees, and screwdrivers into another pocket. I tell myself that as soon as I get home, I'm getting out the gear bags that always accompany us to tournaments and putting this stuff away. How silly to be dragging all of this stuff around in my purse. Soon enough, it is time to head out to get my three sons to practice, so I finish up the coffee, put the magazine away, making a mental note to myself (never did get that paper) to put a real pen in the purse and a piece of paper, and out the door I go, toting my heavy, clutter-filled little bag with me. I pick up my sons and take them to practice. While practicing, an older friend comes in and begins fussing with his compound bow. He doesn't have his tool box. "Hey, Lorretta," he says, "Do you have some tools I can borrow?" No problem, Mike . . . let me get my little purse out. What do you need?

The Top 10 Ways to Know You
Are a True Archery Mom

10 You not only know the difference between *Fast Set Glue* and *Super Glue*, but you have the appropriate glue with you at all times.

9 You know that the thread you carry everywhere does not come with a needle, because the thread is not for sewing, but for nocking point tying, a more important purpose.

8 You have at least eight golf tees or matt pins with you at all times.

7 You not only have a multi-tool, but carry both metric and standard Allen wrenches, too.

6 Instead of change, you carry nocks of all sizes, colors, and brands.

5 You carry small, portable screwdrivers at all times, both standard and Phillips head.

4 You know the weight in grains of those break-off points at the bottom of your purse, and know which kid they belong to.

3 You can put together a *Cavalier* finger tab in less than 15 minutes.

2 Your young archers can at any time say, "Mom, I need . . ." and you can find it within minutes (located in your purse).

. . . and the number one way to know you are an Archery Mom:

1 You don't mind that your purse and your life have been taken over by archery tackle. In fact, you love it.

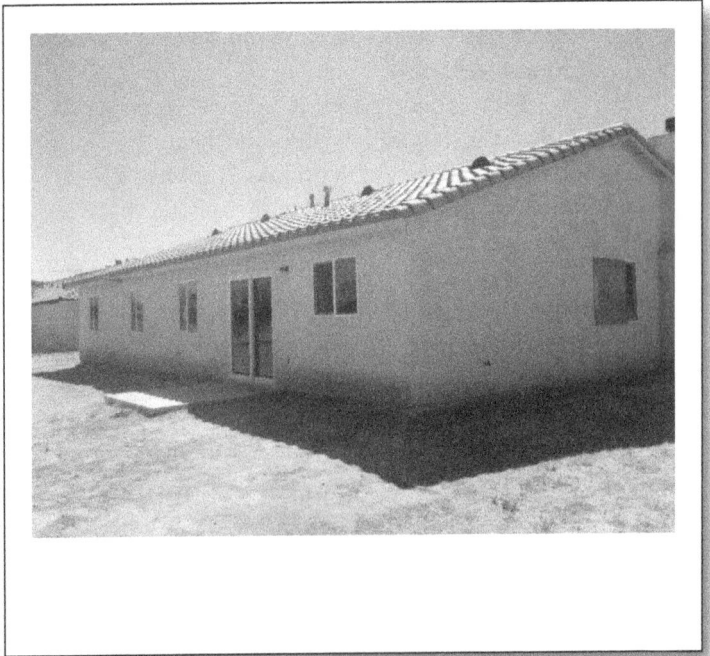

◎③◎

Archery and Real Estate— Getting the Priorities Right

In late 2005 we moved from Utah to California and found ourselves back in the house-hunting business. This is not something we have had to deal with for a number of years. Finding a house is hard enough. Finding a house when you are deeply involved in archery is a whole different matter. Now, before you wonder why I would write a chapter on real estate for an archery book, let me explain.

I'm an Archery Mom and I have priorities.

In Utah, we had access to one of the nicest indoor 18m ranges I've ever seen. With 20 marked lanes, 15 foot high foam matts stacked and rotated on a regular basis, and lighting that can be adjusted for various considerations, we always had a great place to shoot in inclement weather. To top it off, we could shoot for free if we volunteered our time at the range. Since we practice five and six days a week, volunteering saved us considerable money as well as let us "give back" to our sport. We also owned six acres of former farmland. Being archers, not farmers, we had converted it to a full archery target range. After our first year in archery, we bought a bunch of used *Whitetail* target matts from Idaho. We marked off the distances with stakes, had targets for every Cub, Cadet, and Junior distance and even held outdoor tournaments at our house. My sons were able to practice distance shooting, go in to cool off (or warm up depending on the season), eat lunch, go back out and finish practice whenever they wanted. It was ideal.

Then we moved to a hot, dry, and very windy area of southern California. There were no indoor ranges within 100 miles of us and we did not have a large enough piece of property for a practice range (yet). Having been seriously spoiled with a great indoor range and now having essentially nothing meant we needed first to find somewhere to shoot, especially in inclement weather. This priority, of course, came before worrying about how many bedrooms or bathrooms a house would have. This priority came before caring whether there was a patio or not. This priority came before worrying about almost everything most people needing real estate would think about. But then, we already know, I'm not normal. I am an Archery Mom. Have nocks, will travel . . . but need a place to shoot.

We also needed to be able to set up a place to "distance shoot" on a permanent basis. Out here in the hot, dry desert the only grass you see is where someone has a small postage stamp-sized lawn. We will have to shoot amongst the mesquite and sage bush, standing in the searing heat and dirt. The sands blow with the slightest breeze, and "breeze" is not a word used for the air currents here. The word "wind" doesn't do it justice either, often blowing up to 80mph, and a "normal" wind seems to be in the 30-40mph range. Talk about wind shooting! When the wind and the sand blow, well, it's not a pretty picture. Add the summertime heat of 120°F by noon and you really have a good picture of miserable conditions or, rather, you have a good idea of our extreme training conditions.

When we first relocated, we decided to rent while looking for a house on property. We quickly discovered that the realtors didn't understand us. They were unable to find us a suitable house for renting, never mind suitable for buying. You see, our priorities are different from anyone else these realtors have worked with. We needed a practice range. We needed to be able to shoot inside in inclement weather. We needed an appropriate house!

When we first arrived and started looking for rentals, we went from house to house finding nothing acceptable and unable to explain the dilemma. We never explained our intentions because, obviously, we were going to rent and we decided it would be prudent to be quiet about our favorite sport and our need to practice, uh, indoors. We knew they wouldn't understand. They would have visions of whackos running loose with bows and arrows. They would envision holes in the walls. Frankly, they would think we were crazy. But, no one needs to know the truth.

From house to house we went with the rental list, sometimes knowing as soon as we drove up that the house won't work because the lot was too small, or the layout of the house didn't provide a long inside distance. I would go through the kitchen to see if I liked it, and then basically distract the realtor while Bob paced off the hallway, paced off the garage, or paced off the yards.

One day while looking through several rental properties, the realtor commented to me that she didn't quite understand what we were looking for. She had shown us some very nice homes and we hadn't wanted any of them.

She wondered out loud, in a nice way, "What was wrong with us?" On that particular day, we were standing inside a lovely home with a wonderful and fully landscaped back yard. It was so full of trees and shrubs and flowers that you could measure off the grass and patio area in 5 steps. "Yes, it is lovely, but, it won't work," I said, the yard was just "not adequate." She was baffled. The yard was paradise, especially in this desert.

We wander inside the next house and the garage is enormous. Bob and I get excited as he nods to me, which means "keep the lady busy while I pace this off." Then I see him pacing between the master bedroom, down the hall, through the garage door and into the garage. He comes and asks me what I think about the kitchen. This I know means it's a good measurement. "The kitchen? Oh, it's great!" We now have the potential of an "indoor range." I tell him the backyard is quite small and ask him if he could perhaps see about the side yard. He goes outside as I chat with the realtor and continue to distract her from my husband and his weird habit that she has noticed of him walking hallways, walking through rooms, not seeming to care at all about anything other than how long things are. He comes in and quietly tells me that it would be a stretch, but from the front yard, through the gate into the back yard is 30 meters. We would still need to find somewhere for distance shooting but this is a good start. I try to keep my excitement down as I tell the woman that we are very interested in a long term lease of this house. She wonders out loud if I want to go through the rest of it, and I tell her no, if Bob says it's okay, then it's okay. The kitchen is nice and I really do care about that. We make arrangements to return to the realtor's office to complete rental agreements.

As Bob and I get in the car, we are both excited as he tells me that there is an easy 18 meters plus standing room inside the house and though the boys will have to be careful outside, they are good enough to master the narrow gate that they must shoot through between the front and back yards in order to get 30 meters. We are ecstatic! I had no idea what the bathrooms and bedrooms even looked like and I didn't particularly care! All I needed was to secure a place to shoot when the summer temperatures hit 120+°F and the winds that come up nearly every afternoon would not interfere with our archery!

We signed a nine month lease and told the realtor that we were very interested in purchasing a home, but it had to be on acreage and the lot must run from south to north. She didn't ask why, and I was relieved because I hadn't quite thought up a reason yet since I didn't want to let on that we would have two boys shooting up to 400 arrows a day in the house she was about to rent to us. She asked how many bedrooms and baths and I tell her "three and two" would be nice, but we are willing to consider alternatives especially if she could find a long ranch house. She nods and I know she was thinking we are the most difficult clients she had ever met. I happily sign the lease papers knowing part one of this new journey is taken care of.

We were still several months away from finding our dream home. Out here in the hot dry desert, "dream home" may be a misnomer. I miss the green (though not the snow) of Utah. I miss the deluxe indoor archery range at Cache Valley's Hunter Education Center and my JOAD program. I miss the weekend tournaments at Salt Lake Archery (though not the three hour round-trip drive). I knew the realtor thinks we're crazy, but I don't care. I knew my priorities are right. I knew I needed a big ugly piece of desert property to build a new practice range and a long ranch house for shooting down the hallway into the garage during inclement weather. What else would an Archery Mom think of when looking for California real estate?

◎ 4 ◎

Wind Practice

"Aim off, Barrett!" The arrow flies and is a miss.

"Aim further off!" An arrow flies and hits the 5-ring.

"Aim at Grandma's house, Barrett! Go ahead, aim at the house; it'll be okay!"

My 15-year-old son is giving me "that look." I've seen it many times before. Heck, I've already seen it several times today, but this time it is a little more than the usual look of, "Okay, she's not only probably crazy, it is an undeniable fact now." All moms know that look; I just seem to get it more than others. I'm okay with that; I probably am certifiable, but I'm also determined to teach Barrett to shoot in the wind—any wind.

Every serious archer knows you have to get wind practice. Seems like most archers I've come across loathe it, and not a lot of them actually force themselves to do it. We're different. We know that. At our house, we practice in whatever weather we can get, and we never seem to get enough wind

23

practice. That must be the reason we moved to one of the windiest areas of the United States. We must need wind practice. And we can't hunker down shooting in the rental house every day if we expect to have "tournament-like conditions."

When we lived in Utah, we did a mock trial competition one weekend that coincided with the 2004 Arizona Cup. I looked up the weather conditions in Arizona the night before and I told the boys that we would be doing a tournament in tandem with the Arizona Cup. It was early April, we still had eight inches of snow on the ground and temperatures were reaching a high of 50°F, if we were lucky, but that wasn't what the boys were complaining about. "Mom!" yelled my then 15-year-old son Clarke, "It's too windy! This is horrible, I can't get my arrows flying right. This is too much wind! It's not a fair comparison!"

Stubborn as I am, I told them, "Tough!" I told them it was windy in Arizona and it was raining, so the snow on the ground, the cold temperature and the wind were equalizers. They would shoot just as we had planned. They asked for "bonus points." Nope, we don't do bonus points. They asked for breaks. Nope, we don't do breaks outside of those called for by tournament procedures. They asked if I were crazy. Yeah, probably. I asked them if they were intending to be champions or not. That stopped the whining in its tracks. They knew they intended to be champions someday in the not too distant future. They had national dreams, they had Olympic dreams, they had world team dreams. They got the point and kept shooting. It was only after we finished that I looked up our winds for that day—40 mph wind speeds with gusts up to 60 mph. They were furious . . . then they laughed, "She really is crazy, but look how well our scores compared to those from Arizona and they didn't even have half our wind."

Wind shooters, that's what I want, and that's what it takes to win in many competitions. I take no excuses.

Today the wind is ripping at 40 mph. I know this and take Barrett out to my parent's house to practice anyway. Why? Well, for starters, the wind blows all the time. If I waited for non-windy days, he wouldn't get much practice. We now live in the California high desert. Wind is normal. High winds are normal. A breeze out here is 25 mph, a moderate wind, like today, is 40 mph. A high wind is when it's 60-80 mph, and we see those fairly often. I'm not talking about occasional gusts, I mean 60-80 mph steady winds, sometimes for days in a row. I figure, if you can shoot in this wind, you can pretty much shoot in anything. And I'm asking Barrett, at this very moment, to prove it.

He continues to look at me with apprehension as he yells back to me, "Mom, are you saying to aim at Grandma's house? Are you crazy? She'll kill us if I take out her window!"

"Yes! Aim at the new window she just put in, that's probably about right. The wind is so bad; it'll push you pretty far." I am confident that this is right, yet I find my heart thumping harder than usual at the fact that I just told Barrett to aim at the new Low-E, $1000 window my parents just had installed. She probably would kill us, but we won't know for sure until we try it. I momentarily pause to consider what I am saying, and then I nod my head to give him the go ahead. I hope I'm right.

The arrow goes flying down range and hits the 9-ring. Relief rushes into Barrett's face and I am guessing that I've given him the biggest adrenalin rush he's had in a while.

He looks through his spotting scope, the tripod of which is anchored to the ground with a rope tied to big rocks, and seems satisfied with the result. He looks back again while pulling the next arrow out of his quiver, "Mom! You are crazy, you know, no matter where that ended up!" Yeah, buddy – but look at that, you took a huge risk and it paid off. Now, stop fooling around and get busy, we have a FITA round to score, and I hate standing out in this wind.

Lorretta Sinclair

◎ 5 ◎

What's a Little Heat When You're Having Fun?

Since we began in archery in 2002, the hottest tournament we attended was the 2004 JOAD National Championships in Georgia. It was over 90 degrees and extremely humid. Dakota had gotten sick despite my having continually forced fluids down him. It had been a long time since we had been in real heat. We'd moved around the country but hadn't been in heat like Georgia for a very long time.

Most people think Georgia heat was "real heat" as did I, until I moved back to the California high desert. This was the wake-up call. This was the reminder. Georgia was nothing compared to 120 degrees of hot desert sun. Now, we're back and living in real heat. When I lived here before I used to laugh when people would say, "Yeah, but it's dry heat." Trust me, once the desert hits 110°F and you are standing in it, it's tough to match, humid or not.

Barrett and I are sitting outside my parent's house, where we practice these days since we have yet to find our piece of "desert paradise." I'm having a hard time acclimating to the dust, the wind, and the desolate brown of the desert. I regularly reflect on the green, the trees, the

29

ocean of Rhode Island, and more recently the green and the rain of Utah but I try to keep the snow scenes out of my head to make it seem that I left Paradise. Hey, it's my fantasy; I can leave the snow out if I want to.

It's 10 AM and we still have another round to shoot. We should really get out here by 6 AM, but neither Barrett nor I are morning people. We could get out here by 7 AM and things would be more bearable, but that too seems earlier than we can manage. So, if we are lucky, we make our way out by 8 and the suffering begins by 9.

We are drinking water by the liter and it doesn't quench our thirst. We're halfway through a case of the stuff. We wear as little as possible in an attempt to keep cool, though I've yet to resort to a bikini. I don't think Barrett would go for it. I think he'd tell me to get dressed, but the thought of how hot I am invokes all kinds of ideas. All I know is that heat rash is miserable and I'm going to figure out something. I consider that I could hook up a swamp cooler and let it blow, never mind it would blow into the hot desert air. If we stood right in front of it, we'd be cool momentarily. My husband calls to see how practice is going, and we complain loudly. We tell him we need a hut with air conditioning in order to survive. He tells me we should just get up earlier. I tell him I'll be looking forward to that insulated, cooled hut by next summer. In the meantime, I tell Barrett we have to get through *this* hot, miserable summer.

It is now 11 AM and my shirt is dripping wet from sweat. Barrett has taken to alternating between drinking his water and dumping it on his head. He looks up at me with a pained look and mutters, "It's so frigging hot out here, no sane person would do this." Oh, come now, who said we were sane? We're an archery family. We practice in "whatever" and today, well for the next four months, "whatever" is searing heat, wind, and blowing sand. The chance of a cool breeze or a beautiful light rain is zero to nil to zilch. It ain't happening. So we suck up the weather we are delivered. "Shoot, I'm too hot!" I yell. My impatience is getting the better of me as I sweat more and more, my tongue starting to feel like it's three times its normal size and as dry as sandpaper. "Hey! You're lucky, at least you don't have to shoot in it. You get to sit in the heat!" he retorts. "Yeah, well, I don't think it matters what we are doing. It's hot either way, so please, I'm begging you, shoot so we can get the heck outta here!"

It's noon, it's hot, it's scorching hot and we are finally finished. Barrett and I are both so drained, we move in slow motion as we put everything away and pack it in the truck. Our shirts and shorts both look like we've stood in the sprinklers as we are absolutely drenched with sweat. The water is gone, though I'm certain at least one third of it went on Barrett's head rather than down his throat. At one point, he muttered some words interspersed with "and the sweat running in my eyes burns so bad, it's a small wonder I can see through the sight." Stop yer belly aching: we're archers; we have to be prepared for anything. This is practice for the worst case situations. "No kidding, Mom. Worst case situation. Ridgecrest, CA. There you go, there's a motto for the town." We laugh at our plight and grimace that we actually chose to make this move. What were we thinking?

We crawl into the truck with the hope that

I haven't totally drained the gas out of it from the multiple times we sat in it today to cool off with the air conditioner. Since it's a 1-ton crew cab pickup, it guzzles gas on its own; it doesn't need our help by idling and running the air-conditioner, but it seemed like the logical solution so we wouldn't pass out in this incredible heat. Barrett mumbles out loud wondering how I intend to do this type of practice all summer, and I remind him that if we weren't a couple of "night people" we'd be smart and get out here earlier. He winces and says he'd rather suffer with the heat. That's my boy, don't make me get up early, I hate it. Thank you!

The truck starts up, we have a quarter tank of gas, we blast the A/C and sit there trying to make our bodies work enough to buckle up and go. It's hot. It's real hot. How hot? Well, I wasn't about to tell Barrett because the whining would've been so loud, for so long that it would've made everything worse. So I tell him, "Good job Barrett. I know this is hard but if you can practice in this heat, you can shoot in anything. And just so you know, it's 110°F already . . . in the shade." The look he flashes me is familiar. It's the "You're insane; totally insane" one. I know it well. I'm okay with it.

He buckles up and we head towards our rental house. As we drive down the road, he slowly leans over and opens the glove box taking out a California map. "Whatcha doing?" I ask. "What do you think? I'm finding some place else to live. Only crazy people live here." Oh, yeah, let's find the slice of paradise out here in the California desert where you get absolute ultimate archery practice. Wind, heat, dirt . . . we'll be ready for anything.

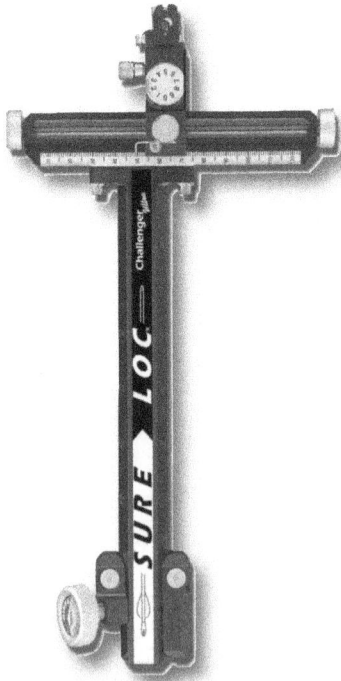

◎ 6 ◎

Learning to Use a Bow Sight

"Hey Barrett. How much did you move the sight?"

"I don't know."

"You don't know? Do you think that was a good idea? Why don't you count this time?"

"Hey Mom, why don't you let me move the sight how I want?"

"Well, frankly because I'm tired of sitting here telling you to move the sight. How about you figure out what three clicks are worth so you can be more accurate?"

"Hey Mom, I am more accurate. I like how I move the sight."

It takes a lot of experience to learn to shoot in various climates, to learn about equipment, to become proficient while having good form. It also takes special technique and effort to master "the bow sight."

My sons have been shooting for awhile now. I grant you that they don't know everything about everything. They are, after all, still novices in the sport of archery. It's only been five years for us and there are many people who have shot much longer who are still learning the ins and outs of archery, so I know I can't expect perfection, and I don't . . . really. But this should be basic!

I love archery. I really do. I don't like this part though:

35

"Your group is on the left. Your group is on the left. Your group is still on the left. Hey! Could you give the sight a few clicks, the group is still on the left. Yeah, well, if you see that, then could you pullleeeaase fix that?" It's days like today when I want to scream.

The practice goes on . . . and on. It seems like forever. It might be forever at this rate. I spend the entire session droning the same sentences: "The group is high."

"The group is now low.

"Did you check that group?

"Did you see where that group is?

"Could you move the sight?

"Did you move the sight?

"Will you move the sight?

"How much did you move the sight?

"Are you sure you moved the sight the right way?

"Well, the group is still on the left, so I'm wondering.

"You're mad? Are you kidding me?

"The group is still on the left. It's been there all day so maybe you like that side of the target, I dunno."

I'm getting "the look." I don't care. I'm actually mad. Ask any of my sons and they'll tell you, Mom getting mad is not a good thing. Avoid Mom getting mad. And I am . . . and I'll tell you why.

The most recently shot group of arrows is in the 8-ring. It's the size of a quarter; it's a really good group. It's been in the 8-ring for four ends. I figured it out on End #1 after three arrows. By End #4, I've had it. Yeah, he's moved the sight: one click . . . one click . . . one click . . . two clicks. Sorry, but at 50 meters, one click at a time isn't going to do it. It's obvious. It's basic. It's making me crazy. This kid is going to make my hair gray in one practice session. I know he's the patient type. Could we have a little aggression please?

Be careful what you ask for, there's always the other kid and he'll make you just as crazy. His groups have been low, low, and low. It's been a left (Kid 1) and low (Kid 2) day. I feel like I'm lost in space somewhere. "Left for you. Low for you." But I did ask for aggression . . . so let's talk about that.

I've heard of the television show "Wheel of Fortune" where contestants spin a wheel to get a prize or monetary amount. But Barrett takes it to a new level. We don't have TV, so I'm not sure where he learned the game of "spin the sight knob" but I can tell you it has the same odds of winning as the TV show. "Move the sight, Barrett." (click, click) "Move the sight more, Barrett." (click, click) "Hey, Barrett, could you move the sight to make a difference?" (Brrrrrrrt) The sight knob spins fast and furious and there is no telling how many clicks were involved—okay, that will move the arrows. Thwomp. Arrow flies out… it's no longer on the left! What a bonus! It's on the right. (Brrrrt) Where, oh, where will the next arrow go . . . no . . . body . . . knows (Brrrrrrt).

"Okay . . . could we get a blend between too careful and too aggressive? Could we learn how many clicks will move an arrow? It's a process boys. You can learn it, I promise. Oh, and guess what? We're not leaving until we make some progress on it."

I don't know why I got frustrated. I don't know why I am still frustrated. Using a sight is a difficult process, especially when it is a very special sight, a unique sight, a sight I paid extra money for. Well, that's what I'm telling these kids who are driving me crazy. I yell out to them, "Hey! Did you know I paid extra money for that sight? Yeah, I did! And I sure would appreciate it if you'd use the special features on it since I paid extra for them! It's a very special sight—it's adjustable! Cost me $50 more just to get that feature . . . for both of you!"

One kid rolls his eyes and grimaces, never mind his groupings; he's the spin the knob and be surprised boy. The other kid, the cautious "one click at a time boy," in all seriousness and innocence says, "Really? They charged extra for it to be adjustable?"

I accidentally spit the water out of my mouth and almost fell out of the chair . . . not knowing whether to laugh or wring necks today. Maybe it's cocktail hour already . . . I could use the break.

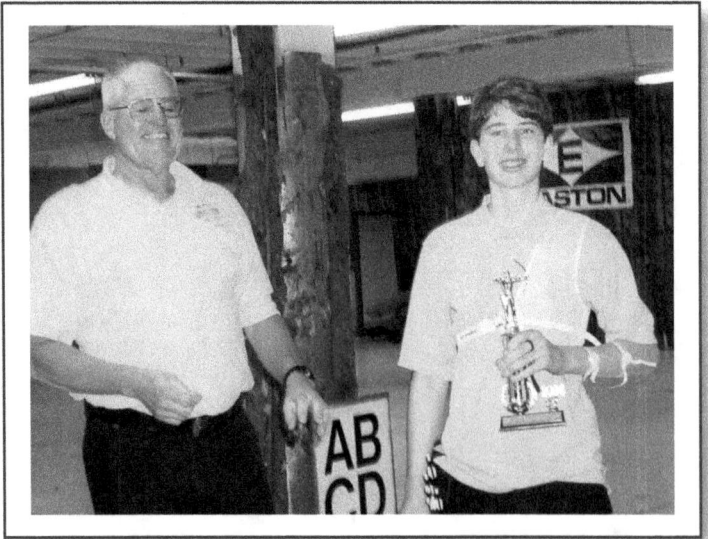

Life Lessons in Archery

The big man saunters back and forth, to and from the target, where he pulls his arrows mostly from the yellow rings of the target, quietly talking, always smiling. He's tall, and from my 4′11″ vantage point, he's really tall. I don't know what he's saying, but his posture, his body language, and his smile tell me it's all very positive and since he's talking to one of my sons, I'm glad I can figure that much out. They are both laughing, and Dakota is nodding his head as the man talks to him.

We'd only been shooting archery for six months when my sons met Ed Eliason. Without even knowing him, his demeanor and mannerisms commanded respect from them. Then he started talking, giving them snippets of information, opinion, and insight. It didn't take long before there was no need to command respect, the boys, then aged 10, 13, and 16, freely gave it to him.

It would be quite a while before we understood that we had one of the *World's Great Archers* giving us pointers. We had no idea he was one of the most accomplished archers in the U.S. We all just liked him immediately.

Sometimes you meet people and you know they are good; you know they are meaningful to you and you want to be around them. Ed Eliason is like that. Every tournament we saw him at, he always took the time to talk to us. He always spent a few moments giving information and insight to Dakota, Clarke, and Barrett. In fact, it seemed like he made a point of it. He always had a smile on his face and we looked forward to seeing him.

After a couple of tournaments, one of the boys commented on how Ed always gave them great words of advice which seemed to be "life lessons" and the phrase, "Life Lessons from Ed" was coined one winter night as we made the 100 mile drive from Salt Lake Archery to our home in Logan, Utah.

Life Lessons from Ed made a difference in the boys' performances at tournaments. We could see that early on. More importantly, I could see the lessons making a difference in everyday attitudes. One of them would say something off-handed and some kid would respond, "Hey, let's keep it positive!"

The life lesson of "staying focused" has come up on more than one occasion. Dakota shot the wrong target in a tournament costing him, at that time, his JOAD Olympian achievement. Ed not only explained the lesson, he then "told on himself" and said, "Everybody has done it. It's what you learn from it that makes the difference." Dakota learned. He got his Olympian Achievement Award shortly after that.

The "Don't let anyone know there's something wrong" lesson is still one of my favorites. When one of them made a bad shot and made no bones about it, to the point that the entire room knew, Ed quietly pulled the kid aside, called over the brothers and said, "Listen, always be positive, never let anyone know something is wrong. If you walk back and forth from that target with a big smile on your face, everyone will think you're shooting 10's. And soon enough, you will be."

It wasn't long after that lesson that we were at a tournament and Ed shot through his clicker, scoring a 6. Dakota and Clarke were on the same target lane, something they had looked forward to (getting lane assignments like that) and were seriously enjoying the experience. Unfortunately, the Marine in Ed comes out at times, leading him to have to learn his own lessons again. The arrow was blatantly in the 6-ring and it was with great surprise that my ears heard words only a Marine can spew so quickly, and then he kicked the post in frustration. Realizing that this amusing tantrum could result in lines down the road of, "Well, Ed did it. . . ," I left my seat and went up to "the big guy" as Clarke often referred to him.

"Hey! Ed, what are you doing?" I asked him with a smile.

"I'm mad! I shot through the clicker and it's down there with a 6!"

"Yeah, well, you can't cuss and kick posts when these boys are watching, what lesson is that?" The huge smile of confidence, fun, and what makes Ed great broke out as he looked down at the kids and said, "Don't do what I do, do what I say. That, boys, was a total lapse of focus." And we all laughed.

I don't know what Ed shot that day, but I do remember the drive home where we all burst out laughing at how our favorite archer lost his cool and we also talked about how quickly he regained his composure and got back to business. A life lesson without Ed present, but a lesson none the less. Dakota and Ed would both share the same tale of "lack of focus" a year later at the Olympic Team Trials when on the same end they both only shot five of their six arrows, proving experienced and non-experienced can make the same mistakes, and they can learn the lessons as well.

As the next 18 months went by, the boys looked forward to seeing Ed and whenever we'd pack up for the long drive home, I'd ask, "Hey, did anyone get a life lesson from Ed today?" and the answer would usually be "Yeah! He told us . . . " and we would discuss the insight and wisdom he provided to our budding archers. I knew that everything Ed had ever told them not only mattered in archery, but in life. Everything he has taught them, all the information he has made available to them, has proven to be true.

In October 2004, we walked into Salt Lake Archery trying to find our way through the toughest "life lesson" of our lives, the death of our son Clarke three weeks earlier. We were unsure of ourselves, unsure of what people would think, unsure that we were doing the right thing. As we walked through the glass doors, "the big guy" was standing there watching us come in and it was a relief to see the smile on his face as he stopped my sons and told them how happy he was to see them. At that moment, I was pretty sure we were doing the right thing, but when Ed wrapped his big arms around me and spoke softly and gently telling me I would survive this, and he was so proud of us for continuing to shoot, for showing up, for doing the best we could, I knew why we cherished our "Life Lessons from Ed." I tightened my grip around him and hoped he'd hold me tight as I knew that with friends like him, I would indeed survive.

Life Lessons from Ed. If you get the chance, get one. It will change your world.

≥●

Ed Eliason has more than 50 years of competitive archery experience. He holds titles as World Champion, two-time National Field Champion, five-time National Target Champion, Pan-American Champion, and 1972 Olympian at the Munich Games just to name a few. Ed also was the pioneering spirit behind the development of Ski Archery. As a Green Beret in Vietnam, he was awarded the Bronze and Silver star. One of my favorite things about Ed is that after many years of marriage, he still refers to his wife Joan as "my bride."

◎8◎
Tournament Time!

Load the car. Drive to the airport. Unload the car. Check in. Get inspected. Get inspected. Get inspected. Finally, free from lugging around the heavy stuff. Fly across country. Gather baggage. Load into rental shuttle. Unload shuttle. Load rental car. Drive to motel. Unload car. Wake up and load car. Drive to tournament, unload and reload car; many times over the next few days. Finish tournament. Load car. Drive to airport, unload rental, load into shuttle, unload from shuttle. Check in. Get inspected. Get inspected. Get inspected. Whew! I'm tired. Feels like all we do is unload and reload. Okay, we shoot arrows in-between, but we will do more heavy lifting than anything else, I'm pretty sure of that.

It's that time of year that we travel back and forth across the country, a family of archers, chasing the tournament calendar. After dragging all the equipment into the check-in line and getting the suitcases out of the way, we drag the bow cases to security so they can be inspected and we can lock them. We've learned to arrive early to perform what now is our ritual when traveling. Everyone has it down on what to do, what to say, and we keep a watchful eye as our cases either make it through the X-ray machine and onto the conveyor belt, or get held up, opened, inspected as we answer the question "What's in this case?" for the security person making the inspection.

"No sir, it is not a weapon. It is recreational equipment.

"No, I do not hunt.

"Yes sir, it's very valuable.

"Yes sir, it's very delicate, and I would appreciate it if you put that back where you took it from.

"Yes ma'am, I do a lot of practice.

"Yes, ma'am, it's a portable canopy for shade. My mom will explain.

"Thank you very much! Have a great day!"

We've had inspections in a variety of places. Once in Ohio, it took place in a back room, where it was quite uncomfortable since there wasn't anyone but the inspector around. I couldn't figure out why we were taken to the back, but it worked out in any case. We've had inspections right in the middle of the floor next to Check-in. I don't know what they would've done if our cases turned out to have contained something dangerous. We were, after all, standing in the middle of the Continental Airlines Check-in area. Then, of course, the more normal inspections were taking place right outside the X-ray machine while we watch them picking through our equipment not having a clue what anything was hoping they don't do something drastic, like want to take a plunger apart or remove the foam padding. Finally, we get the cases locked and on their way, make our way to the boarding area and make the long flight to . . . wherever.

Arriving in Baggage Claim at our destination, we split up with some of us going to find the "Oversized Luggage" area and see what turns up there. It seems that some baggage handlers think our pop-up canopy and bow cases are "oversized," while others put them in with the suitcases. I've given up trying to figure out which does what. We just never know where our stuff is going to end up, so one of us always stands at the carousel. I stand at the carousel quietly hoping that the shade and cases go to "oversized" so I don't have to muscle them off the carousel.

As the bags begin to slide down the ramp, we wait like always, mostly hoping that if nothing else, the bow cases come off. Like all good archers, we've stood and watched suitcase after suitcase come down the slide and remarked, "We don't need our clothes, but we do need our bows." It's always a huge relief when the bow cases turn up. You can always buy additional clothes, but bows are personal. Such a switch from the days before archery when I cared about my clothes thinking I might not have a good vacation if the suitcases were lost. Things change once archery is in your veins. Finally, we are relieved as the big black bow cases turn up.

After everything has been pulled to safety, we gather up our goods and head for the rental car. Dragging two double SKB bow cases, two overstuffed suitcases, three carry-on bags, at least one laptop and the infamous, hard to handle, popup canopy (for shade) through the airport, leaves us appearing nothing short of a circus act.

A baggage handler approaches us with a cart and just as I'm thinking, "Oh yeah, where's my wallet, let's pay him," Dakota waves him off with "Nah, we got it."

"We do? We have it? Are you kidding me? I don't have it, I'm sure. This nice fellow wants to earn some pocket money. I'm all for it," I mutter, scrambling to find my wallet, while the carry-on bags slide off my shoulders and onto the floor almost toppling me over in the process. I think they weigh as much as I do.

"Come on, Mom, we've got it. It's fine," Dakota assures me. And he waves the guy off again. I am so disappointed! Slumping under the weight of "my share" which includes two carry-on bags, one on each shoulder, while dragging one suitcase behind me, I move on reluctantly hoping we don't have to go too far to find the rental car shuttle bus. I'm exhausted already.

The shuttle bus pulls up and we take longer than anyone else to get everything aboard. People are staring at us as we strong-arm things into the van. Well, okay, the boys strong-arm, I stand by acting like I'm actually helping while trying to get the numbness out of my arms from having carry-on bags slung over each shoulder. I try and make light of the fact that people are clearly annoyed that we take so long, explaining that we actually did leave the kitchen sink at home; it's just that we brought everything else we own. Amusing or not, it's still embarrassing to take so long.

When the shuttle pulls into the rental car area, people scramble faster than they did when getting on, in order to get off ahead of us. I don't blame them, so we patiently wait. We are last. Then as the boys begin the process of dragging everything off and stacking it on the sidewalk, I go and get the rental car. As I walk off, I hear one of them mutter, "I hope she gets a bigger car than the last one. I don't want a bow case on my lap again."

Keys in hand, we start dragging the suitcases and equipment to the rental car. "What did you get, Mom? I hope it has a big enough trunk." I don't know, it's some sort of mid-size car. It should be big enough. "Yeah, like the last one? Mom, I hope you didn't get that Ford *Focus* again. Remember, we can't all fit?" Well, since you boys are so smart, I could just get us a minivan, then we'd all fit for sure. How about that? The loud groans accompanied by, "Oh man, don't do that. That's just too old. That would be too embarrassing," make me laugh out loud at them. Such stylin' critics, these sons of mine.

I get a high-five when they see it's a midsize SUV and they are happy that no one has luggage in their lap for the one and a half hour drive to the motel. I've passed yet another Archery Mom traveling test. Never mind it took me four or five tries, in the eyes of my sons, to "get it right."

Getting through a tournament, with the early mornings, long days, ups and downs of having multiple people competing, the highs, the lows. . . . It's all a big drama; sometimes it is fun, sometimes it's not, sometimes I wish I had stayed home. Sometimes I do stay home and send Dad instead. The tournament ends, we pack up, head for the airport, and arrive home again. Well, after more heavy lifting, more dragging heavy bags, more inspections, more strange looks and comments, more scolding from my sons about how I never keep up and I've got the lightest load. Hey! Did you ever realize I'm the smallest person and maybe it's hard for me to keep up? I don't say that out loud.

By the time we load the car for the three hour drive from LAX to the high desert, I have gone full circle from, "Oh, it is great that tournament season is here," to "I loathe tournament season" to "Okay, this wasn't too bad, I can do it again." Good thing I go around in the circle, because a few weeks later: load, unload, inspection, inspection, inspection . . . load, unload. . . . It's the circle of my life these days.

Lorretta Sinclair

◎9◎
True Grit

If you're old enough, you probably think this chapter has something to do with John Wayne and one of his western movies. Sorry, it doesn't. Though maybe it's worth watching one of those movies just to get into the mood of dry desert heat, wind, and blowing sand. That would set the tone for sure.

We're not a normal family, we know that. We don't even try to pretend we are, there's really no point. But, our stories of trials and tribulations don't always seem believable, so I continue to write the facts, just the facts, so others can learn from our valuable experience.

Equipment maintenance is a very important aspect of archery. Every time it rains, we pull our bow's limbs out of their pockets and dry both the riser pockets and the limbs. We make sure the limb bolts are dry and the detent buttons on the limbs are dry. We take the plunger off, take it apart and dry it, too. And then there is the bow sight that also needs our attention. Keeping everything in good working condition is extremely important.

Removing grit from your equipment is a form of equipment maintenance known mostly to those of us who live and shoot on a regular basis in the wind and dirt. Why would someone do that? I dunno, but we do. There are other people who do this; we're not totally alone in our insane little world. What we have learned could turn out to be very helpful advice for those of you going to compete in, say, the Arizona Cup where the wind always blows, the dirt field wreaking havoc with your equipment. Lucky for most of you, though, it's a once in a year event, as opposed to those of us who deal with it on a daily basis. The expertise we have at grit removal is incredible.

Take for instance our Alpen Optics spotting scopes. When it rains, we wipe them down, pull out the rings on the front of the scope and dry the inside of it, and put it in the case. But when we shoot in the wind and dirt, things get tricky. When we have a damaged scope and take it to Alpen, we find ourselves apologizing, a lot, as they look at the damage and then turn the knobs and everyone in the building, and probably on the block, can hear the grit that sounds similar to fingers on a chalkboard. "We clean them, we really do," I assure the folks inspecting our expensive spotting scopes. I know Alpen doesn't believe us and why should they? They can't understand our shooting conditions until they see them, but if they ever did, they'd use us for the next Alpen commercial announcing to the world, "Our Alpen optics survive not only the Extreme Conditions of the Mojave Desert but *the Sinclair family*, as well." And then they'd show video of our 40 mph "moderate" winds and the sand blowing across our archery range slowed only by the sage brush that it passes over as dust devils and whirlwinds form sucking up anything that isn't tied down. Oops! That's giving away how two of our scopes got damaged.

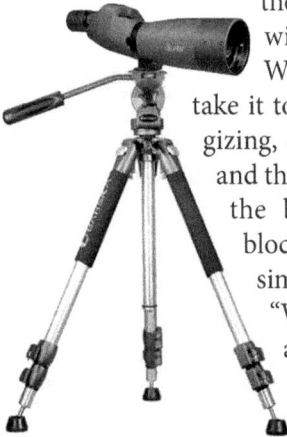

Yeah, there's that commercial again and now it has visuals and, worst of all, it's all true!

When our cushion plungers start acting funny, you can count on "grit" as opposed to rust being the problem. Fact is, it doesn't matter what kind of plunger you use, they all fail in the Mojave Desert when trying to work against the element of grit. We know this as we've used them all. Bow sights don't fare any better. Once the grit is caught in all those knobs and screws, we are in quite a mess. And new meaning is brought to the question of "Can you please move your sight up or down; left or right?" Because a lot of the times the answer is, "Well, no, actually Mom, I can't. The sand was blowing all during practice and since we practice in dirt, sage brush, and mesquite bushes, it really is quite impossible at this moment to move any knobs on any part of my bow, least of all my sight." We all agree that would be handy, though, to be able to move the sight. We need a solution. A hermetically sealed sight perhaps?

Taking off the stabilizers and V-bars at the end of many practice sessions, we can clearly hear the sand grinding inside the threads of the boys equipment. It is sickening as they unscrew and take apart everything. My ears tune to that sound in a matter of nanoseconds now, as I cringe at what damage is probably occurring and realizing there is actually nothing I can do about it.

Ah, the reality of desert shooting. A reality of wind and grit. You know we practice in the wind, but we also practice in "the grit." We practice in swirling dust devils that form as the "breeze" (ah-hem) that blows on a near daily basis crosses the valley floor. For some reason, these are seen for miles and always seem to take aim at us as we stand out practicing, minding our own business. We use a lot of colorful words when that happens. As we watch them bearing down on us, we have a few seconds to cringe knowing there is no way to grab everything and run for safety. And then the dust devil grabs everything: target mats, stands, spotting scopes, and water bottles; everything that isn't nailed down. Uh, okay, the target mats, stands and scopes were nailed down, but they aren't now! Gosh darn it (replacements for the colorful words I really use), we keep forgetting to put everything in the truck in spite of having been caught in these nasty, torna-do wannabes before. Is it hope that keeps me from doing it? Naiveté? Forgetfulness? Something is awry because I continue to leave things out in the open and then I pay for it as I scramble after the dust devil waiting for it to relin-quish our belongings, even our 8′ x 8′ canvas shade. Give it back! I insist! Those 122 cm target faces cost me $6 a piece! I want it back!

Because there's only sage brush and sparse mesquite bushes to even slow the wind down as it smacks against our legs, slaps us in the face, stings our eyes, and covers every inch of our equipment in grit, I realize that, basical-ly, we have to put up with this condition. That's why we are experts at grit removal. And we also don't lubricate or oil anything. We learned that, our way . . . the hard way.

I promised Alpen I would never forget to tie the Alpen scopes down again after that one day where we lost both of them in one fell swoop. And I've kept my prom-ise; I just want them to know. I couldn't promise to keep the grit out. I just can't figure out how to do that. Well, unless, we give up the extreme training conditions that we have set ourselves in; the conditions that will help create world class archers by virtue of the fact that in Barrett and Dakota's opinion, "It can't get any worse than 120 degree

heat, sand blowing in our faces, and winds raging any-where from 40-80 mph." We've already lived in snow that stays on the ground for five months of the year and tem-peratures of minus 30. We've also lived in New England where it rains until saturation and 12″ of water accumu-lated in our basement. We've been through hurricanes. We have actually, I realize, seen it all. So their opinion on "the worst ever" is undoubtedly quite accurate. We could, I suppose, move somewhere else. Barrett is leaning over me as I type this, saying, "Yeah! Let's get a map! Let's get going!"

Naw . . . what fun would that be? I wouldn't have any-thing to write about!

Lorretta Sinclair

Photo Courtesy of Steve Ruis

58

◎10◎

Traveling with Shade

Outdoor season finds us traveling all over the country for U.S. Archery Team (USAT) and Junior Olympic Archery Development (JOAD) tournaments. It's not enough that we come with baggage. Stop laughing, I mean suitcases . . . sheeesh. A carry-on per person, two bow cases, and multiple suitcases would be enough for most travelers, but then there's "the shade" that makes things even more interesting.

Viewed as "possibly dangerous" by many airline employees, "the shade" (our pop-up canopy) has had more than it's share of security screenings. Standing in

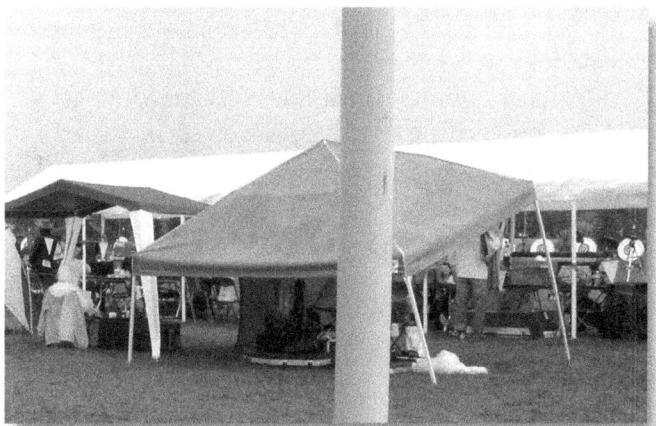

line explaining the bow cases, the need for locking them and then waiting for them to pass through the X-ray machine has always been an adventure. But getting "the shade" on and off a plane has often left us with a story to tell. First, there is the explanation to the airline security person.

"Ma'am, what is this?"

"It's a shade."

"A shade? What do you mean it's a shade?"

"It's a sun-shade; you know a canopy, like a tarp to keep the sun off of you, like for picnics and such."

"Oh, are you going to a picnic on an airline?" Ha, ha.

"No, we're going to an archery tournament. We will be out in the sun all day for four days and so we take shade with us."

"Well, if it's shade, why is it so big?"

I feel my eyes rolling and hope the guy doesn't see it. I feel like one of the boys when they have one of their, "Ohmigod our mother is making me crazy moments." And just like one of my sons, I answer the question even though it is ridiculous.

"Uh, well, it has a metal frame, then the tarp goes over it, and then we sit under it."

"A shade, huh? On an airline? Go figure."

I'm resigned now . . . I'm involved in yet another meaningless conversation about "the shade." It's unbelievable how much I have to discuss it.

"Yeah, I know . . . it seems odd, but really it's quite necessary."

"Okay, well, we'll put it through X-ray, and then you stand over there in case we need to inspect it."

I already know how this is going to go. "In case we need . . . " really means "Get ready to have it pulled from its carrying bag and inspected." What do those anchoring metal stakes look like going through that X-ray machine? And since the concept of "shade" has escaped the security clerk, how can I expect it to get through the screening without being "inspected"? They are so curious; they're going to pull it out, no matter what.

"Uh ma'am, could you stand over here while we open this, uh, this shade?"

Good thing we came early. I've been here before.

Unfortunately, the shade companies don't make cover bags to handle extensive airline travel. The cheap, thin nylon bags are worth about one trip, maybe, and that's if you are lucky. We learned our lessons traveling with "the shade" long ago when it came off the airline carousel hanging out of its shredded bag, stakes coming off one by one, and the extra side tarp stuck in between someone else's suitcases. The hammer never did turn up. That experience prompted several changes when traveling with "the shade."

First, I bought some heavy canvas; more commonly used for camping ground cloths and made a new bag. I reinforced the bag by sewing extra canvas in the corners and on one end to help keep the legs and ends from ripping it, hoping it would last at least one season, if not more. Then, covering the bottom of the legs with cardboard and taping them to further minimize possible damage, taping the ground stakes and hammer to one of the legs so they weren't flopping loose in the bag and finally closing the draw string and taping it tightly with packing tape. These changes significantly helped with traveling. However, the now tightly clustered metal stakes must make it look like an even more dangerous item as it passes through the X-ray machine. I don't know, perhaps it looks like little missiles or something, ready to be

launched. What I do know, is with these changes, I've at least been reasonably sure it will make it through the flight, but the last stage of taping the drawstring closed has made security unhappy with me when they want to check out this shade I claim I have.

"Ma'am, you know you really shouldn't tape things up like this. We have to be able to get into the bags for security purposes." This, I'm being scolded about as the man is ripping the tape from the end of the bag.

I am silent, though my head has quite the conversation: "Yes, I am aware that I shouldn't tape the bag closed. I'm also aware of what happens when it isn't taped closed. So I tape it and hope against hope that someday someone will let me through the security checkpoint without ripping it open. After all, I am becoming well-known in some airports I frequent. "Oh look, there's the lady who travels with her sons and "the shade," they say nudging each other and nodding at me as if they have an inside track on some kook flying around the country with a weird bag.

"Ma'am, did you hear me?" The security inspector brings me back to reality. "You shouldn't tape it up like that; it's too hard to open."

The boys are standing watching me to see if I'm going to comment or not, and then biting my lip, I stand there twirling the roll of packing tape around my fingers, wondering how he's going to react when I explain to him that now he will need to retape the bottom for me because I'm not about to leave it open. Thinking of all the things I could say, I decide to try and get him to be nice and retape.

"Uh Sir, you see, if we don't get the shade safely to it's destination, my sons and I will not have any way to keep out of the sun. Where we're going, it's 90 degrees, hot, humid, and sunny, and the boys are competing in a tournament. We really need the shade to show up intact. I realize this is a pain, but could you please retape it for me? I've got the roll right here."

Looking at me perhaps as though he's imagining it, he slowly comes over and takes the tape from my hand. "Ma'am, you really need to figure out some other way to do this."

My mind is reeling, I'm biting my lip, and I at least keep this part of the conversation in my head: "Sure, you tell me how and I'll do it. No problem. You guys are the ones who keep inspecting the thing. I tell you what it is, but you just can't help yourselves."

He slowly rewraps the bottom of the shade and sends it on its way. We thank him profusely, and move on ourselves. I feel his eyes rolling at me even though my back is now turned toward him. It doesn't matter; we got the shade through security.

Arriving at our destination, we patiently wait for everything to come down off the plane, and gather it up heading for the rental car. One of the boys comments on how the shade looks like it made yet another trip unscathed. I remind them, we haven't unpacked it yet.

The shade takes more than its share of airline beatings. I think they give it an extra beating "just because."

The shade has become our problem child. First it is difficult to maneuver in and out of rental car trunks, which leads to the boys constantly telling me I get too small of a rental car, and they always point to the shade as the issue. It is cumbersome, heavy, and a pain, but then I remind them how nice it is to be able to sit under at tournaments.

The next morning as we set up for official practice, we busy ourselves first with the shade. One leg is slightly bent, and in the top framing, another slightly bent bar. This is "no biggie" as the boys straighten them out to get the cover on and we hammer the stakes into place.

The hammer, which we used to forget, now travels taped to one of the legs like the stakes do, and is worth the strange looks from the security people and the comments like, "ma'am, that's just funny taking a hammer with y'all." Yeah, okay, ever try pushing stakes into the ground in dry Georgia clay with your foot? A hammer gets it done. I've gotten defensive not only about the shade, but about the stakes and hammer as well.

We finish staking the shade down, put the chairs under (at least they supply chairs otherwise we'd have to figure a way to bring some), hang the side shades, which include our Pirate flag and a banner for Clarke's Memorial Scholarship, and then we are finally ready to enjoy a weekend tournament. Ahhhhh, shade. It is a necessary component of our travels.

The tournament ends and we are ready to make our cross country flight once again. On two occasions we have had somewhat bizarre endings to the "traveling with shade" odyssey. In Georgia at the USIAC tournament in

2005, a wind whipped up and grabbed the archers' tents that were not secured to the ground and flung them over a four foot chain link fence straight at us as we stood under our secured shade. Running to get away from the flying mass, which included quivers full of arrows from the Stanford Archery Team which had gone to lunch, we managed to grab the bows and equipment, and turned around to see our shade completely crushed, lying on the ground under the archers' tent, which was thoroughly entangled with ours. That same year in Colorado Springs, the "replacement shade" purchased after USIACs, was crumpled in a similar fashion, leaving only the tarp useable. On these two occasions, the destruction of our shade left me with ambivalent feelings. On one hand, I didn't have to drag the infamous shade back through security. That's a real plus in my opinion. On the other hand, I had to buy a new one. Replacing two tents in such a short time span was not the most economical way to spend the season.

Worse, at USIACs, the archers' tents were destroyed, so we not only went and bought a new one, we then gave it to the archers to use, which left the rest of the family standing in the sun! A love for archery is not always good for us.

The "normal" ending is more economical but a bigger hassle. At the end of the tournament, the boys pack and rebag the shade, as usual. Arriving back at the airport, the security adventure that we know all too well begins again. "Uh ma'am, what's in that long bag over there?" "What's a shade?" "You know that's oversized." "Bring that on over here and then security might want to inspect it."

No, you don't say!

◎ 11 ◎

An Archery Mom's Guide to House Cleaning

When you are an archery family, there are unique issues that find their way into the most common parts of your day, such as house cleaning. The extenuating circumstances you find yourself in can often be comical or frustrating or both! Take house cleaning. (Please!)

I'm a little slow sometimes. I admit it. It's not often that a person has unidentifiable "stuff" stuck on their stove or counter top. Usually, as the cook, I pretty much know what I've done in the kitchen and can account for sticky juice, stains, boiled over potatoes on the stove, you know, normal things that get spilled on a stove or counter.

But, we're an archery family—learning all the time. So it shouldn't have been a huge surprise (though for some reason I did not have that "ah ha" moment for quite a while) when after many times of scrubbing the stove top and wondering "What is this clumpy stuff that is stuck to the stove?" I had a moment of clarity one fall day (the boys will say "a moment of sanity" and they'll say it was very brief but whatever), it occurred to me that this junk stuck to my stove and counter was—Oh, freaking, duh— Hot Melt Glue!

67

Bob and the boys have been taking arrow points out and cementing them back in using "hot melt" over the stove's open flames since I can remember. I hadn't put two and two together, but now that I had, it needed to stop. I mean really, who has to use a razor blade on their stove and counter tops to get little round blobs off?

Stomping upstairs to my computer, I typed and printed a sign in big black letters. The sign was a reminder, a rule, an order from the cook which was expected to be followed. The black and white sign hanging above the kitchen stove, in bold print, clearly explains, "No Hot Melt – Go outside!"

I was so tired of the mess all over the burners and stove top that I kicked them out – not once, not twice, but regularly. I thought somebody would listen. . . . I even explained to them that there were no less than four (4!) propane torches in the garage and it really was no big deal to step out there and take care of one's arrows where no one really cared if they dribbled, drizzled, and globbed hot melt onto the garage floor.

The sign remained up for a year – and I kept finding clumpy globs on the stove top. It's truly amazing that it kept happening too, since everyone swore, "It wasn't me!" whenever I asked the question, "Who used hot melt on the stove?" followed with, "Get in there and clean it off!" I kept hoping the sign would make an impression on someone, anyone. Alas, it did not. It simply drove them into denial.

The months wore on and certain persons thought they were being sneaky but I kept finding globs of hot melt on my stove, so it was more than a little obvious. I'd yell out to no one in particular, "Stop using the kitchen for points! Go out to the garage!" and then I'd take the razor blade out and scrape the hard clumps off the stove. Some days the "offender," whoever that might be that day, would forget and leave the stick of hot melt on the counter, or worse, the actual points. So when cries of innocence echoed back to me, I knew better. It's not very sneaky when you leave behind the evidence!

It became a contest of who could use the stove and would they get caught. I wouldn't have minded if they'd just stop leaving the mess behind. But no, they were always in a hurry to take old points out or put new ones in and get out to practice. It never really occurred to anyone that Mom would know they'd used the stove in spite of the boldly posted sign that now one of my funny men had scrawled underneath the "No Hot Melt," the words, "Why not?"

Vacuuming is another example of an Archery Mom's unique situation. The pops, clunks, and sputters of the vacuum as I roll over the floors of what seem to have become the "archery area" of the family room were unknown to me before 2003.

I admit, I'm over 50 so my eyes aren't as good as they used to be. And so I have learned, as an Archery Mom, that vacuuming without contacts, it's a wonderful thing. Really! I urge you to try it. You can't believe how it de-stresses your life when you can't see the things you are vacuuming up. You know you hit a nock when the vacuum clunks and sputters. You know you hit points when the noise sounds like a brick just came through the window. So really, why look at it all—if it doesn't get sucked up in the vacuum, okay, maybe someone will pick it up.

In my case, however, the only person who apparently picks up is ummm . . . me, the Forever Archery Mom. Unfortunately, it took me awhile to figure out what that black stuff was on the carpet and why it was so hard to vacuum up. I'd vacuum and go back and think, what the heck? I think one of the boys finally said, "Mom, geez, it's just the black tape from our spin wings. We stripped the arrows and that's black tape that got stuck on the floor." Really, that's how it works around here! No one even gets excited that there is black tape stuck in the carpet and I can't see it until I put on my contacts.

Bending down to rip the tape which is now firmly stuck to the carpet from people walking on it, I start to ponder how much extra house cleaning archery actually causes me.

Bows in the middle of rooms that must be moved, along with bow cases, spotting scopes, quivers and whatever else gets dropped on the floor as archers come in and out from practice as I try to clean. Counters and stove dribbled with hot melt, black tape in the carpet, along with nocks, points, and the usual assortment of archery tools that were left behind. The dining table is, at this moment, covered with a scale to weigh points and arrows and over by the entry door is the arrow saw surrounded with carbon dust as the boys lean over it cutting arrows. Yes, truly, as I type this article I am witnessing arrows being cut in my entry way.

"Ah-hem, isn't this what a garage is for?" I inquire. Uhhhh, no. It's a hot summer day and no one wants to go into the hot garage to cut arrows so they brought it inside and declare, "But mom! We put it on the tile so it wouldn't make a mess!" Really, they said that. They actually thought that!

Trying not to laugh out loud at the comedy of my life when trying to clean, I finally sit down on the floor and lean against the sofa. Quietly I watch the boys resume cutting arrows in the entry way. Something keeps poking my head and I keep pushing it away, distracted by yet another mess in the making. I push whatever it is again, and finally after the third time, I roll my head back to look—the cats are playing on the sofa with a spare bow string. It's tangled up and around one of the figurines on the table next to the sofa and the cats are having a field day. Every once in awhile, the end of the string gets swatted near my head. The mighty 'thwack' of the cat as she hits me upside the head while chasing the end of the string urges me back to work.

The boys are now done cutting arrows. They did put the saw away . . . but wait, what are those round things laying on the floor? Arrow shaft remnants, left especially for me to pick up. How lucky I am!

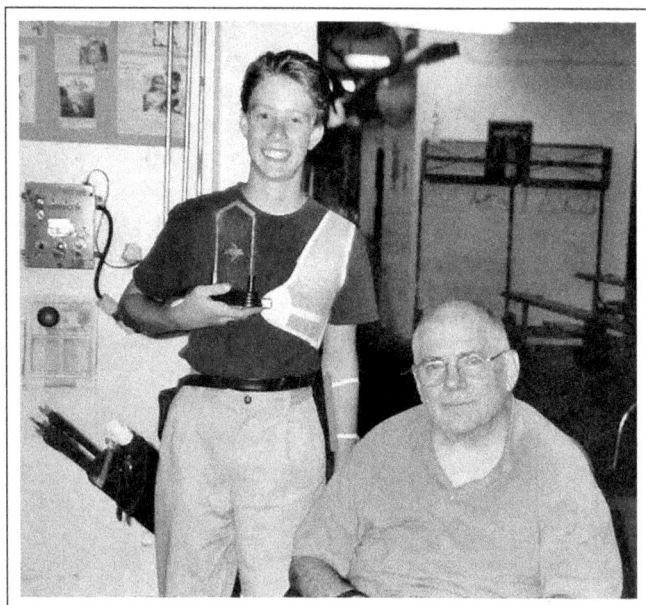

◎12◎

The Money Pit

"Mom . . . I neeeeed. . . ." Oh, gee whiz, here we go again. Some kid "needs" something, "needs" something archery-related. Go figure. Archery stores should give me discounts—big discounts. There should be a point system for spending gazillions of dollars, something akin to the "frequent flyers clubs;" and we should get "frequent buyer's points" worth discounts on our next purchases.

This is all Larry Smith's fault. Really. I'm sure of it. He owns *Salt Lake Archery*. The man sold us our first sets of equipment for all three boys. He knew what was going on. He's been in archery a long time. He saw the stupid "addicted to archery" looks on our faces. He should have told me it's a money pit—it's only fair!

But no, instead, he sat in his wheelchair patiently teaching my sons to "Open your hand and let the arrow go" addicting them to the feeling of loosing an arrow and watching it hit the yellow. He even cheated on that! He did! He had them standing at five meters when he addicted my family to archery! Where's the morality in that? I ask you, is it fair to smile while young children learn to spend their parent's money? Larry did!

And he's been in the shop or at the range when he's heard the whine of "Mom, I need . . ." and he didn't bat an eye. No sir! He didn't stop those kids and say, "No sir, you can make do at a national competition with that Bullseye bow and Easton *Jazz* arrows." Oh no, he encouraged them. He kept teaching them to get better and better . . . and he would add fuel to the "Mom, I need . . ." fire by saying things like, "You know Dakota, you are now ready to try a stabilizer . . . or a clicker, or a different plunger . . . or to get new arrows." Whenever they improved, I heard the "Mom, I need . . ." signal and now, here I am, with more receipts from Lancaster Archery Supply, Salt Lake Archery, and Jake's Archery than a mom ought to be saddled with. I have folders of receipts . . . and the once occasional, "Hey Mom, can I get that new arm guard?" which was only going to cost me a few bucks, is now, "Hey Mom, I just have to have those X10 arrows, oh yeah, and I really need the tungsten points for them" and all along Larry just smiles. Hmmph. There ought to be a sign on the man saying "I addict your kids to archery. You are soon to be broke."

It's not all Larry's fault, I'll grant you that. Those dog-gone boys did research when they decided to compete nationally. They discovered Spin Wings, carbon/aluminum arrows, and Beiter armguards, nocks, clickers and plungers. They found the best of the best. Clarke had outgrown his *Bullseye* bow only six months from the time he started. Then I thought I'd gotten lucky buying a used Hoyt *Gold Medalist* riser and limbs for $100. I had gotten lucky, because his next bow, a Martin *Aurora* with Hoyt G3 limbs, cost me almost $1000! It was a "Mom, I just gotta have it" moment. The words should be banned— "Mom, I need..."—just banned. That's the only solution. Ban those words and stop Larry Smith from teaching my sons to get better at archery!

Then it became Mike Gerard's turn. He's almost as guilty as Larry. He taught the boys how to make their own bowstrings. Learning this wonderful thing, turned the universal lament into, "Mom, we need string making materials!" Oh, we couldn't just buy some plain, white string and some serving. Nope, Mike introduced them to "And look, you can each make a custom string with the colors you like!" Yeah, like I needed that. I went from buying bowstrings from Salt Lake Archery at $16 a string to buying spools of BCY thread in red, green, blue, yellow and black and serving thread in each of the same colors!! Mike taught them a skill that day, and he cost me a fortune. I just love him.

Then along comes the adolescent growth spurts. Arms got longer and Larry says, "I hate to tell you this, but . . . they need new arrows again." Yeah, sure, right, you *hate* to tell me. Now I know why he is always smiling. What did those boys do to set this up? Go in the back of the shop and get on the arm stretcher? Egad, I just bought new arrows a few months ago, why does he have to keep growing? And I have to do everything in threes. You can't buy one Beiter armguard in the "special" color of blue for Clarke, without buying a red one for Dakota and a green one for Barrett. Nope, if one gets an armguard, they all (miraculously) need a new armguard. It's an archery miracle. Need a cushion plunger? Pull out three, please, because if we "just have to try" a Spigarelli plunger to "see" if it's better, then we have to try three!

Not long ago, I overheard a dad talking to his wife at an archery tournament. They were new, I could tell. They were almost as clueless as I was when we first started. The mom was asking the dad about why some of the kids had black arrows, whilst their kid was shooting some purple ones and inquiring as to whether her son might shoot better if he had the black arrows. The dad replying, "Nah, those are just people with a lot of money to throw around. We don't need those expensive ones to hit 70 meters next year." The mom nods and says, "Whew, I thought this might be an expensive sport after all."

Now, I admit it; I was eavesdropping. I don't get a lot of laughs at tournaments these days, so hearing something so incredibly funny was really tickling me. I wanted to pull my chair up into their tent and revel in the sublime bliss of their ignorance. And it was all I could do to keep myself from falling out of my chair laughing and sarcastically retorting, "No! Archery, an expensive sport? Heck, all we do is buy some "bows and arrows;" that doesn't cost much!

That poor mom has no idea what's about to happen. Her boy hadn't even gotten to the competition-level bows yet, never mind competition-level arrows. The dad reassuring her that the rest of us "were rich and had money to throw around" ought to check out my Visa card! It's a revolving card—it revolves around archery shops.

Sitting there laughing hysterically at how soon they will understand their reality, I did a quick run down for just one son and his equipment (and he's the cheapest of the lot):

One Boy and his Bow(s)
April 2002
Bullseye bow and aluminum arrows, armguard, finger tab, beginner sight, small portable case - $136 out the door
From Oct 2002 until August 2004
Risers: *Gold Medalist* riser and Martin *Aurora* riser
Limbs: Hoyt wood, Martin limbs, Vector limbs, different Vector limbs, Hoyt G3 limbs, different G3 limbs
Arrows: aluminum Easton XX75 *Platinum Plus* to *Vector* to *ACC* to *ACE* to *X10* (many dozens of each)

Plungers: Cavalier to Spigarelli to Beiter
Stabilizer: 24″ to 30″ to 32″ plus V-bars
Sight: Beginner to Shibuya to Sure-loc
Fletch: inexpensive plastic to Spin Wings at $14 a bag
Armguards: Gotta have those $12 Beiters
Tabs: $3.99 dog hair tab to $30 Win&Win tab
Cases: SKB single, Aurora double

Then of course, there is the backup equipment—in case anything goes wrong at a tournament, you need an entire duplicate setup!

And multiply that times three!

I love archery, and it's a good thing, because all my expendable income goes to this "inexpensive" sport. It's a money pit . . . and someone should have told us so!

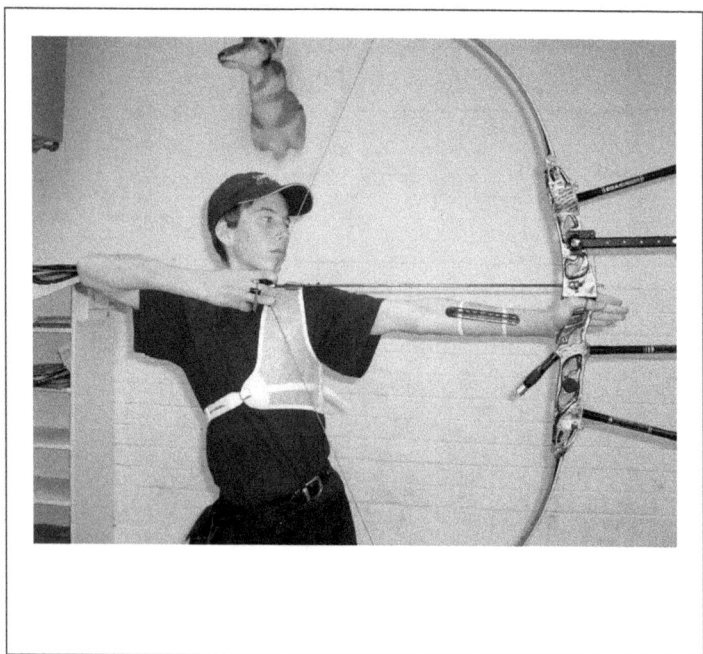

◎13◎

Be Humble . . .

Learning archery in Salt Lake City proved to be an excellent place for many reasons. Not only did we have a great indoor place to shoot at Salt Lake Archery, we were surrounded by people who are "big" in archery. Coming into the sport without any knowledge of either the history or of the actual physical aspect of the sport, we were in a word, naïve. It would take us a while to sort things out and as we did, we were amazed by the people who regularly came in and out of Salt Lake Archery. We did not know who they were, because they did not brag, boast, or "let you know" that they were either accomplished in the sport itself, or a part of the top people working for leading manufacturers, like Hoyt and Easton. Heck, we didn't even know Hoyt and Easton were based out of Salt Lake City. And when we did become aware of that, it meant little to us because we were still in the "beginner bow" stage and had not yet learned that Hoyt and Easton were top-notch companies.

But then, again, we are the people who started in recurve archery by telling our then 13-year-old son Clarke on his birthday, "Choose whichever bow you like and we'll buy that one." We were much more than naïve, we were totally clueless.

So, it was over time that we would meet people, chat with this or that person at tournaments, have someone

79

come and tell us, "Wow, Clarke has a great release," or just watch people watching the three boys, without ever knowing exactly who these people were. What we saw were some really nice people who came to the local tournaments or to the range to practice. Even when we started to grasp the names and their association to archery, such as Techmikov, Eliason, Barrs, McNail, Gillingham, Gerard, Wilde; my opinion stayed the same because of the way they came and went: unassumingly.

We had been shooting archery for a little over two years when Clarke made the 2004 Jr. World Team. It was a goal he had set for himself and he worked hard to make the team. He knew he didn't have the same long-term experience as most of the kids trying out. But what he lacked in experience, he made up for in determination. When he made the team, it was one of the most exciting moments of his life. He had practiced in snow, wind, a hail storm (literally), freezing rain, and heat six days a week for months and he had given everything he had to achieve his goal. He was not only excited about being on the Jr. World Team, he realized that he was good at archery.

It was with some surprise, as we were driving into town for errands a few days after he made the team that he said, "Mom, I've got a problem."

Uh oh, I thought, getting braced for who knows what. To this day, and for the rest of my life, the conversation that followed not only made me proud, but helped me understand some of Clarke's uniqueness. "Okay, what's up?"

"Mom, I'm really good at archery."

"Yes, you are."

"No, Mom, I mean, I've been doing some research

and reading, and I am really, really good at this."

"Yeah, I know, we started figuring it out when we saw people watching you shoot; people we had no idea who they were and then those same people would smile, shake their heads, and some of them have said to us, 'He's really good.' I get it Clarke; you are really good at archery. So what's the problem?"

"Well, um, I'm struggling because I know I'm really good at this, and I'm having a really hard time controlling my ego. That's the problem. I am really good and I'm going to get even better, but I don't want to be a jerk. I don't know what to do."

Stunned into a rare silence, we drove for a few miles while I tried to regain my thoughts. My 15-year-old son understands something that a lot of successful people don't get in a lifetime. More importantly to me, he is sharing it with me and asking for guidance. I am stunned and proud and not real sure what to say, and then a moment of clarity comes. . . .

"Clarke, remember when you had only been shooting archery for eight months and we went to the Utah Open? You went over to the crowded practice bay and you were the only kid over there. Everyone else was an adult but you weren't intimidated. You worked your way in to practice and ended up next to a left-handed guy. Remember shooting next to that guy and how he was talking the whole time to one of his friends and yet hitting the 10-ring shot after shot? Remember how you liked walking back and forth from the target and enjoying how this guy complimented you on where your arrows were hitting? Remember how he told you while he was looking at your target, 'Hey, you're pretty good.' Remember how you told us later, 'See that guy over there? He told me in the practice bay I had a really great release.' Do you remember all of that?"

"Yeah. . . ."

"The guy was so normal, so unassuming, so fun to stand and shoot next to, that you had no idea who he was, right?"

"Right."

'Then, my advice is simple, Clarke. Whenever you feel that your ego is getting the better of you or you think you are going to be a jerk because you realize how good at this you are, just think back to that first time that you stood next to Jay Barrs and remember how humble he was, how unassuming, how you would have never known until someone later told you, that this man was a two-time Olympian and an Olympic Gold Medalist. Be humble Clarke, like you saw Jay Barrs be that day. If you do that throughout your life, you will never be a jerk."

After a bit of silence, Clarke responded, "It's really hard and that's why I was worried, but I can do that, Mom."

"I know you can Clarke, because that is part of what makes someone great; being humble when you don't have to be. Jay Barrs could've told you who he was, he could've bragged and boasted, but instead, he complimented you. He told you he liked your release, he complimented your shots, he made you feel like you were important. That is all you ever have to do, remember that day in the practice bay."

We drove the rest of the way into town talking about the day that we finally did realize who exactly Jay Barrs was and we laughed at ourselves and our naiveté.

Two weeks later we were sitting at JOAD Nationals in Georgia. A man and his son came by our tent and asked me if Clarke would be willing to have his picture taken with this young man. I told him that when Clarke came back from lunch, I would be sure to send him down to their tent. As I explained to Clarke that a boy named Matt would like to have his picture taken together, Clarke rolled his eyes at me and laughed nervously, "This is embarrassing mom! Why would someone want their picture with me?"

To which I responded, "Because you're good, because you're nice, and because you have the lesson of being humble. Get moving." I watched my lanky, shy son uncomfortably wander down the line of tents looking for the man and his son. When he came back from taking pictures he said, "That wasn't so bad. They were really nice to me."

We left Utah without me having ever met Jay Barrs. We were never officially introduced. I've spoken to him briefly. I believe I was a tournament registration person when that occurred. He just comes in and out of Salt Lake Archery like any other person, to shoot. But, Jay Barrs, without ever knowing it, made a lasting impact on my son. And I thank him for that.

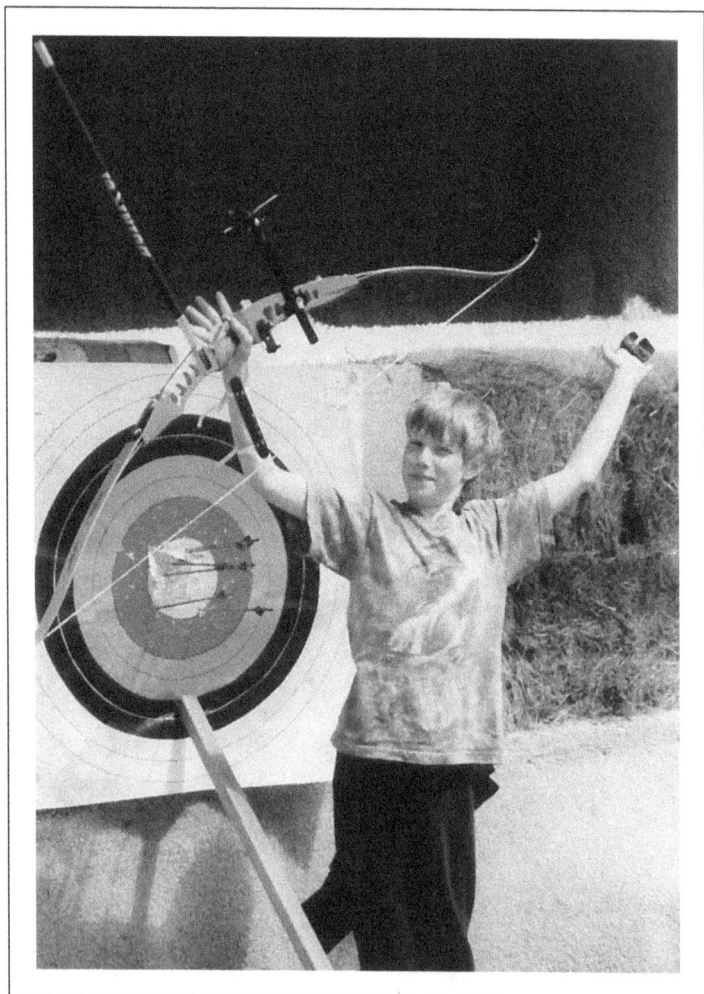

◎14◎

Telling on Mom

"Hurry, quick! Grab the camera and come outside! Barrett just shot ten straight 10's from 50 meters! Hurry!"

My husband Bob has bounded through the door yelling at me to come see a wonderful feat by my then 13-year old son Barrett. His excitement is catching as I get up from my computer desk and try to make sense of his somewhat jumbled words as he enthusiastically tells me how he just watched Barrett shoot a perfect 100 point end. Shooting from 50 meters as a Cub is the longest distance Barrett had to shoot, so ten straight tens is a moment of glory.

It's getting dark and excitedly I grab my camera, slide my feet into my sandals and head for the door. Bob is waiting for me on the porch and is all smiles as we bound down the front steps out to the archery field. Barrett is standing by his target beaming; a smile so broad and wide that it excites me even more. I stand and look at the target and manage, "Wow!" "Wahoo!" "This is great!" and other exclamations of my excitement. For the next five minutes, as Barrett stands by his target with ten arrows clearly in the 10-ring, I click away with my camera, giving him all the deserved accolades; telling him how wonderful this is, how amazing, how. . . . Hey, wait a minute . . . that smile looks a little odd, his eyes are kind of glancing towards his dad . . . what's up here? I pause for a moment and try to

85

make sense of this funny look on my son's face.

"Barrett! Did you really shoot all those arrows in the 10-ring?"

"Yeah, Mom, I did! Dad was standing right here next to me!" Now the smile gets a little stranger, perhaps a bit too big and the eyes are darting a little faster. I look at my husband and ask the same question. "Did he really do this?" With a straight face, I am assured by my husband that he stood at the shooting line watching Barrett as he shot his last practice end and they closed up with ten shots, all landing in the 10-ring.

And then . . . no longer able to contain themselves, they both burst out laughing. "Ha, ha, Mom, you were so excited, you should see yourself! You should hear your-self, you were talking so fast and how many pictures did you take because that camera was clicking away . . . ha, ha."

Well, I'm not laughing. Getting an Archery Mom all excited by ten 10's at 50 meters and faking it is hardly a laughing matter. My heart was pumping so fast, I didn't even realize it until I was ready to box their ears for them. All moms live to see our kids do well at something, achieving goals and pushing themselves to greater heights. Whether it's school or sports or creative activities like pottery, drawing, and painting, moms get excited when their kids succeed. We really get excited when our kids do something extraordinary. Shooting ten straight 10's from that distance with Barrett's 26# draw weight was a huge feat.

Truly annoyed, I told them that this stunt was absolutely not funny . . . but they were still laughing. Going in for dinner (Yes, I did feed them, even though they didn't deserve it.) they continued the banter the whole time we were eating, torturing me by recounting my expressions and excitement.

After enduring their harassment for quite a long time, I leaned over to Barrett and said, "Do you remember the story "The Boy Who Cried Wolf?" Do you remember how I told you over and over as a little boy that it was important to tell the truth? Do you remember how no one believed him because he told them things that weren't true? Well, buddy boy, someday you will shoot ten 10's in a row and I won't believe you." Undaunted, Bob and Barrett just laughed even harder.

The lesson of "The Boy Who Cried Wolf" came sooner than expected. The following day, Barrett shot six 10's from 50 meters into his target and told me all about it. But, I didn't believe him. I told him he did the same thing as the day before; moved the arrows around on the target, stuck them all in the 10-ring, just this time his dad wasn't around to be in cahoots with him. I told him I know he stuck them in the 10-ring when he went down to retrieve his arrows. I told him I wasn't about to embarrass myself again by getting the camera and taking pictures. I lectured him thoroughly . . . and then, the last laugh was on me once again. Barrett stood with a smirk on his face and laughed as he matter of factly said, "But, Mom, I haven't gone down to get my arrows yet and you are standing right here watching me shoot, so you know I just shot six perfect 10's because you were spotting them through the binoculars." And with that, he went off to get the camera for me so I could take 'legitimate' pictures of his latest feat.

As he hopped up the porch steps, I yelled after him, "Yeah, well, no one will believe you even if we have the pictures since your new name is "The Boy Who Cried Wolf" and I'm going to tell everyone what you and Dad did to me!"

Pausing only long enough to flash me the biggest smile he had, he yelled back, "But, Mom! I am a phenom!" and disappeared into the house.

I took the pictures of Barrett and his perfect 60 that day. He didn't deserve it. He laughed and made fun of me the whole time, recounting the day before and how now he had not only played a great joke on me, but followed it up with a "real 60." Then he called his dad so they could laugh some more.

Bob's version of "what they did," of course, lays it all on Barrett. They both explain, "Well, we did close out practice with ten arrows: seven of them were tens and three were in the yellow." Then they deviate: Bob says Barrett looked up at him with mischievous eyes and said, "We could really get Mom with this. If you go in and tell her I shot ten 10's, she'll believe you." And so the plan was hatched. Barrett, of course, and still going by the name of "Boy Who. . ." denies it all. But he does have a very mischievous smile as he does so, so who knows what the truth is.

Bob has been after me for a long time to write up this story. He keeps telling me how funny it is. I didn't want to because, frankly, it's embarrassing to be hauled outside like that on such false pretenses. To be told your child is phenomenal, only to discover it was a joke. To get all excited about some arrows in the 10-ring.

I only wrote this because, well, after three years of sitting on it, I guess it is kind of funny, but only kind of funny. And to tell the total truth; I've made fun of Barrett in so many articles, I figured telling on myself was just fair play.

Actually, I should have named this chapter, "Dirty

Rotten Scoundrel Boy and his Dad;" that would have been more fitting.

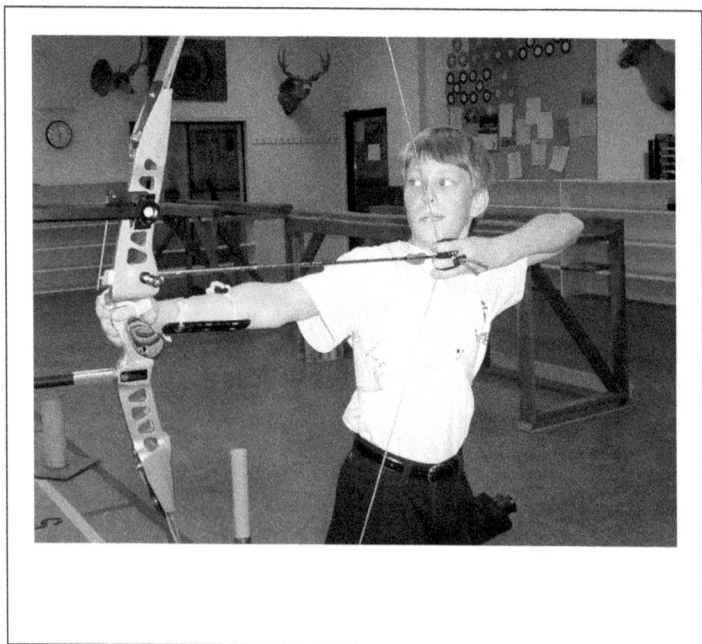

◎15◎

The Art of Staying Focused When Things Go Terribly Wrong

A friend once remarked that watching archery was "as much fun as shopping for a baby stroller." Okay, color me weird, but I liked shopping for baby strollers, and I like watching archery. I find it to be intense, exciting, and full of life lessons.

As an observer, not an archer, I have watched the grace and skill of archery as well as the anxiety, stress, and sometimes poor sportsmanship of competition. I have learned much as an Archery Mom, a coach, and an observer.

I have watched young archers come off the shooting line in tears from sheer frustration from things not going well in a competition. I have witnessed a highly ranked youth archer drop kick his quiver across the shooting line when he lost an Olympic Round match, and I have been surprised as a world renowned archer kicked a post and uttered words we won't repeat here, when he shot through the clicker and scored a six.

I have also seen grace under fire from my sons when

91

they didn't know I was watching. I have observed an archer with jet lag shoot the wrong target and calmly remark, "Well at least they were all 10's." And observed hard fought OR rounds and knew that the "loser" was disappointed but impressed by the handshakes at the end of the matches. One time, in Las Vegas at the World Archery Festival, I watched a young recurve archer as he maintained the *Art of Staying Focused When Things Go Terribly Wrong* and learned yet another lesson from archery and Barrett.

On day one, by end seven, Barrett had shot 21 out of 21 yellows. On end 8, he seemed to struggle, having to let down two times. On the third let down, the arrow slipped from his hand and landed in another competitor's target. As I watched, I knew that this could be disaster or triumph, and only he would tell the tale. There was a brief look that crossed his face of "What was that?" and then he finished the end with two nines. As he walked back to the sitting area and approached me, he asked, "Where'd the first one go?" and when the answer was, "It's a miss. It's in the other kid's target," the reply of "Well, the next two were good shots" was the answer I would hope to hear from my archers. It was the attitude that we should all strive for when things go wrong and we can't undo it. At that moment, I was reminded of how often I could manage my own frustrations differently. Barrett had just set the bar high.

As the archers went down to score their arrows, I again watched, thinking that this young man could still lose his focus after the zero settled in to his thoughts. The potential for trouble was still very real. I was impressed as he returned to the shooting line, giving no hint that he had just given up his chance to finish in first place that day. His posture, his smile, gave no clue to what had just happened. Only those who had been watching him and the competitors on his target knew what had happened because his behavior led you to believe he had just shot all tens. With six remaining arrows, he stood up to the pressure of his mistake and shot, two 9's, and four 10's. Grace under fire from a kid.

There have been many books and articles written on how to handle competition pressure, how to focus, how to deal with problems that could throw you off your game. Many seasoned competitors find it difficult to put into practice the wise words that they read. Many never master this important part of competition. And I know of some who don't even think you have to have a "mental game" to compete. After going through so many tournaments with the boys, I now know that having a mental game is imperative for both mother and son. And staying focused and on track when things go wrong, even if you know that first place is now unattainable is the difference between a winner and a loser in the game of life.

Watching archery may be boring to some, and it can be difficult and stressful if you are an archery parent. It can also be full of lessons in life as well as archery, sometimes learned at the hands of a kid who triumphs instead of losing focus. Barrett walked out of the tournament having shot 59 out of 60 golds, that "0" was the only arrow to miss the gold. He left holding in his hands a second place medal which I know was disappointing but not the end of the world as he proved to me that day. We can all learn a lesson from that.

◎16◎

Bow Tuning –
Whew, Who Knew?

My son Clarke is standing at the shooting line stomping his foot in frustration and I have no idea what is going on other than he keeps telling me "The arrows aren't going where I'm telling them to and it's not me!"

I'm looking over at the boys' JOAD coach who is patiently watching them shoot. Larry Smith has patience unlike anyone else I've ever met when it comes to observing kids and archery. He slowly rolls his wheelchair over to where my husband Bob and I are standing and says, "Clarke needs new arrows."

"What? I just bought him new arrows a few months ago!"

"Yes," Larry says, "but he's grown and he needs new ones." Arrgh. You've got to be kidding me. It's not long before I hear the same phrase, this time it's about Dakota, "He's grown, he needs new arrows."

Then Larry rolls by us again, "Oh, I hate to say this, but he needs a different string. When we're done, we'll get a different one for him."

We get Clarke set up with new arrows and a new string, things turn around and he's happier because now they are "going where I tell them to." Oh, I think, wow, he must have used up that last string from all the practice!

Whatever . . . that's that and we are all set. Think again.

One day, the boys are reading through one of the archery books that we have purchased and they start talking about this thing, this "bow tuning." I look at them in utter confusion, "What's bow tuning?" They aren't sure, so I tell them "Well, when we go to JOAD this week, ask Larry."

In the meantime, the boys are giving me new words for my vocabulary: fishtailing, porpoising, tuning a bow, arrow flight, weak arrows, stiff arrows, front of center balance, plunger offset, forgiving tune, unforgiving tune, draw length, true draw length. . . . On and on with new terms, phrases, and sentences that I had never heard before. And they are confusing and I'm wondering, what the heck are they talking about?

Within a few years of being in archery, I almost sounded like I knew what I was talking about. But just "almost," because if you had more than two years of experience, you knew that I was still just an archery neophyte, but, hey, I was trying!

We head out for JOAD and Clarke and Dakota make plans to talk to Larry about "bow tuning" while I silently wonder what this is going to cost me. We arrive at Salt Lake Archery and the first thing that pops out of Clarke's mouth is, "Hey Larry, can we tune my bow?"

Instead of an answer, he gets a question back, "What do you think bow tuning is?"

My ears perked up, 'cuz this is my question and while the boys could not explain it to me, they definitely knew something was up and I wanted to know, too.

Clarke shrugs his shoulders and says, "I don't know. I read in a book that you can tune your bow and if you are competing, it's important. So can we tune my bow?"

Larry doesn't give in easily and lobs another question back, "Well, what did you learn from the book?"

Clarke: "That there's a way to get more points if you tune your bow."

Larry: "You can't buy points."

Clarke: "Well, I want to tune my bow, so I can get better scores."

By now, I am frustrated because Larry isn't answering questions, he's just lobbing them back and I'm not getting any useful information from this back and forth exchange. I want to know about this bow tuning thing. Larry ends the conversation with, "Why don't you read some more and come back and tell me what bow tuning is and what you think you need to do and then we'll talk about it."

Aaarrrghh! Are you kidding me? I have to wait to get important information while my kid goes and reads more to give you more info so you will help him? Now, I am going to have to go find this information just to satisfy my own inquiring mind!

Clarke was not happy that night as he wanted to "tune his bow" whatever the heck that meant. He wanted higher scores and he wanted them in whatever way he could get them and he wanted them now. He was putting in the practice time and he figured if there was a way to get more points, this bow tuning thing was a way to help. Miffed at not getting the immediate help they were seeking, both boys determined to get the answers.

Dakota and Clarke set out reading through the books and started telling me all about "bow tuning" . . . and I ended up more confused than ever.

"What do you mean that you can 'tune the bow' by changing the number of strands in the string?

"What's this weak arrow, stiff arrow stuff . . . they're arrows, what's the difference?

"Weight of the point? It's important? Why? Oh geez, back to that weak arrow, stiff arrow thing.

"And the fletching matters, too? They'll fly differently with different fletching? Are you serious? Who said that?

"The plunger is screwed into the hole on the riser, what do you mean by 'offset?'

"Centershot? Huh? The arrow is coming out of the center of the bow, what are you talking about?"

I am beginning to see the picture: cha-ching for the archery store . . . and not so good for my Visa card. No wonder Larry was coy and forced those boys to learn more about bow tuning instead of just telling them.

Number 1, there's more to tuning a recurve bow than can be stated in five sentences on a JOAD night. And there's more money involved – at a time when I was up to my eyeballs in buying equipment as these boys "upgraded" from beginner to intermediate to advanced equipment. And since I did everything in three's, it wasn't cheap.

And now . . . this "bow tuning" thing . . . egad. I should have received a degree for what I learned about bow tuning.

Clarke and Dakota studied all week, reading the archery books, online researching, trying to find anything they could about this mystical "tuning of the bow." The Easton Arrow chart was now installed as wallpaper on our computer monitor's screen. And a "We Need" list was sitting on my computer desk: arrow points (various weights), strings with different numbers of strands, fletches of various types and sizes – plastic vanes, feathers, Spin Wings . . . Spin Wings? We have wings for arrows? Man, those suckers are expensive . . . do we really need them? Why are you getting three different colors in three different lengths? What do you mean you need to try different ones? Isn't there a "chart" for this?

I am overwhelmed by the information being dumped on me and I'm not sure that it's even true. This "bow tuning" thing, it sounds so much like the Ginsu knife commercials—they say their knives are superior, but are they? You don't know unless you buy them! And my boys are asking me to buy a bunch of stuff to try to make their arrows fly better. No guarantees there Mom; it's all trial and error. I finally tell the boys that they have to talk to Larry. He told them to learn more and get the answers, so bring it up and see what happens. I'm not buying anything until I understand better.

The following week at JOAD, Clarke is excited, because he's going to bring up "bow tuning" and this time he figures he's got the answers to the questions Larry will throw at him.

Barely past the greetings, Clarke launches into it: "Hey Larry, I want to tune my bow."

Larry: "Well, did you find out what that means, exactly?"

And we're off . . . the battle of the questions being lobbed by Larry and Clarke throwing back the answers. Finally, Larry smiles at Dakota and Clarke who have given answers (many of them not quite right but we don't know that until later), but enough to apparently satisfy Larry that they do indeed understand that some equipment changes can effect their scores, but then he admonishes them again, "You can't buy points."

My boys, always looking for ways to better themselves and despite Larry's assertion of "You can't buy points," begged to differ or at least they begged me to let them try to "buy points."

Larry gives us the quick version of bow tuning. Eventually we learn a longer version, then learn multiple versions from others and from reading and a lot of trial and error.

When the boys' arrows are fishtailing towards the target and as Clarke aptly put it, "aren't doing what I say," there is a way to gain points by making changes to the arrows to get them to fly better. The experience level of the archer certainly has a lot to do with the tuning, and when they are new and their form varies widely, it may not help at all.

The quiz session that Larry put the boys through was valuable. It forced them to learn a lot of information and this caused them to put their own time and energy into tuning their equipment as well. Larry's unwillingness just to "tune the bow" because Clarke asked was a valuable lesson. The boys learned to watch their arrow flight for one another and the words that once were so confusing to us became common verbiage. Dinner would often be centered around who's arrows weren't flying right or what changes in groupings a new pair of limbs or new arrows had made and all of the options to try to get better flight.

Bow tuning is a time consuming effort—and when you have three bows to tune, with three archers with different skill levels, the adventure of "bow tuning" can be exasperating as well as rewarding. In the case of Clarke who had become quite consistent in his form, the tuning of his bow resulted in a 50 point increase in his scores with only a few changes. Eventually, when we knew enough to tune the bows ourselves, all of their scores jumped up. And that was certainly worth the pursuit of information . . . and the expense.

We are doing bow tuning—just saying it out loud makes me squirm . . . and smile—we sure have come a long way.

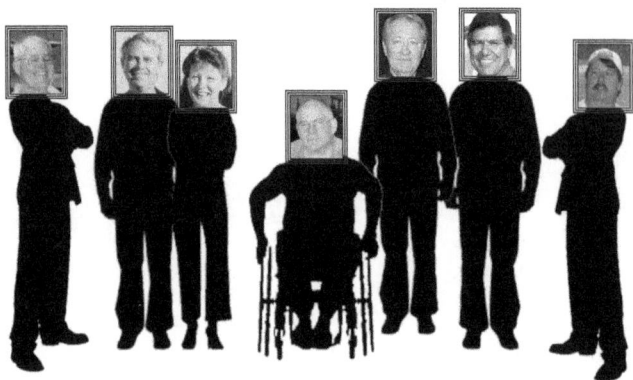

© 17 ©

It's a Team Effort

We all hear the stories and claims when someone does well. It appears that a kid is coached by everyone under the sun. Everyone wants to be involved, a lot of people take credit, and really, when it comes down to it, when someone succeeds in anything it usually involved a lot of people: a team, a major effort, dedication.

Archery isn't any different.

We started out in archery as some of the most naïve people to have ever come to the sport. In some ways that was very good; in others, it left huge gaping holes that had to be filled. Experience to find, knowledge to gather, expert advice to seek and lots and lots of experiments in practice. You can know everything there is to know about archery, but if you can't use it for yourself or impart it to others, it doesn't really matter. And you can be the reverse of that and think the only thing you need to know about archery is that it involves a bow and an arrow but if you have a 30 strand string, under-spined arrows, and are overbowed, you won't get very far.

There are so many people that helped us along the way in our archery journey, some of whom continue to help us. Many have provided us with invaluable knowledge and information that we are grateful for.

Larry Smith, owner of Salt Lake Archery, started our boys in archery. Larry's forte is teaching kids. He started our boys out as he has many other kids and he has always been patient with them. Parents may not fare so well when he's cranky from sitting in his wheelchair all day, but Larry always has a soft spot for the kids. To this day he is someone we count on.

Larry, one of our trusted and valued experts, comes from a great perspective: a wheelchair. He is one of the best observers I have ever met. No, he is *the* best observer I have ever met. One day when Barrett was having trouble finding the yellow on a target and his arrows were seemingly wanting to hit the black and blue rings, Larry sat and watched in silence from his vantage point of the wheelchair. Rolling to the left, rolling behind, rolling to the right, watching shots again and again until finally he says, "Barrett, did you realize . . . " and there in the words would be "the problem."

I once said to Larry, "I can't believe how you pick up the smallest and slightest of things." And he replied, "I've got to sit in this chair, I've got a lot of time to become an observer." And he's right. He can pick up the slightest change in form or see the tiniest last minute twist, pull, or turn to the right as the clicker goes off. The angle of a hand in the bow, the tucking of the thumb too far, the change in the elbow at full draw. Whatever it is, he sees it.

Barrett and I have made the drive back and forth to Salt Lake City many times since we moved to California in late 2005. And this is significant when you realize that it's a 12 hour drive and Barrett thinks driving 30 minutes to somewhere is "too far." But ask him if he wants to go work with Larry and he's packing his case and looking for clothes.

Larry is more than an observer, he stuck with us when times have been hard. When Clarke died, Larry's shop gave us a home, making us feel safe in the archery range and somehow knowing that all we needed was a place to go, a place to be "normal," to fit in and to loose some arrows (or watch them in my case) and never be judged on what we did, how we did it, or the pace that it took for us to come out from the fog of the life altering loss of Clarke.

The thing I most appreciate about Larry is his willingness to watch us come and go, to know that when we think we need to talk to someone else about arrows, or form, or equipment, that he also knows that we appreciate and savor the knowledge and information he has given us . . . and that we will be back. It would be foolish to think we know everything, and it would be impossible to expect Larry to know everything. Different people have imparted different types of information and knowledge to us, but the one person we always come back to is Larry.

As three-time World Champion Rick McKinney once told me, "Coaches are a tool for your toolbox. There's no reason why you wouldn't put as many tools in the box as possible." And in our case, we have a family toolbox. Rick gave us wise advice to put many tools in the box and to regularly evaluate the tools as well. Our team changes accordingly, but we are always aware that it is a team effort.

Bob Romero, at the time I write this, is the Head Coach at the Easton Center of Excellence in Gainesville, FL. Before that, Bob taught and worked with many archers who succeeded in the sport. Bob is a person who exudes a positive attitude to the point that it contagious. Bob taught us more about equipment than I can remember (so I wrote it down). He also taught us to be positive even when things didn't look too great. His willingness to help teach us about equipment resulted in serious improvements in scores. And he insisted that the boys learn what to do with their equipment, which "took" with Dakota but not with Barrett. Dakota is a master with his equipment, which is awesome; Barrett, uh, not so much. He still hands me his arrows to fletch with a smile on his face. It's okay, it's better than the alternative which is to have to refletch them after he has attempted the job. No one would shoot those arrows. But it's not a matter of not knowing how, because we know he knows how.

Mike Gerard taught us how to make strings. It's his fault that I own almost every color of BCY string material they make. It's also thanks to him that Dakota and Bob are master string makers. He generously taught them the ins and outs of that particular and very important art. He also taught us about tabs and little hints and bits of information that only someone who loves archery as much as Mike, who is a total and complete equipment geek, would know. My first trip to a tannery was because of Mike. I learned more about leather that day in Bountiful, Utah than I ever needed to know, but I can pick out a good backing for tabs because of his fun adventures into equipment and his willingness to impart his knowledge on our family.

Dick Tone taught us that a drive to Phoenix, where he lives, was worth the trip. Because of him, we added more tools to the toolbox, including field archery. We also found yet another positive person who gave of himself to help us learn.

Ed Eliason is, and will always be, one of the most incredible people we ever met in the sport. Ed's longevity in the sport and his love of it is one of the best lessons our boys could ever have. Just watching Ed work the room laughing and talking to everyone is a lesson in itself. But for archery, Ed is the master. He's seen it all. An archery lesson with Ed is a lesson in manners, psychology, equipment, and form, oh . . . and a half Buddha smile.

Rick McKinney's sage advice about putting tools in the archery toolbox isn't just for adding coaches and information. It's also true that when something isn't working for you, you need to take it out of the toolbox, even if it is also a coach, which we've also done.

If the goal is to achieve your best, then you have to gather the needed tools and periodically assess what's in your toolbox. We're a team - and we've added and subtracted to the team and the toolbox as the needs change. What we've taken from the past members of our team has been valuable, and what we continue to utilize is immeasurable. We keep the toolbox stocked with the equipment that they each choose, coaches that recognize that this is a family and can embrace that fact, supporters who don't hesitate to help out, and the Visa card that pays for it all.

Bob and I aren't archers, though Bob has toyed around with it a bit. Our focus has been supporting the boys in their endeavor to be good in the sport. Along the way we've met some wonderful people and learned a lot about archery. Bob sits and watches archery videos until we are so sick of them that there are literal groans in the house. But he keeps smiling as he researches and works to gain insight and information that can help our sons.

For myself as Archery Mom I am the part of the team that coordinates it all. I became a certified coach, learned to tie on nock point locators, tune a bow, and deal with difficult tournament folks, learned to observe from Larry, to be patient (I try) from Ed, and to push when things aren't going well from Dick and Bob. I've learned as much as I could to support my sons in the sport that they love. Through the days of shooting in five feet of snow, freezing rain and hail, hot summer days, wind, and sand blowing in our faces, trekking from tournament to tournament, Mom has been the constant. Not that I know everything, because I surely do not, but I also don't hesitate to find someone who does know the things we don't and ask for help.

The toolbox is full of the things, and people, we need and when we need to add or subtract from that box we do so. The boys are lucky to have worked with so many fine people. The team we've created works for us.

Oh, it's his
"Mom."

IF YOU'RE
JUST A MOM,
YOU'LL HAVE
TO STAY
BEHIND
THE LINE.

She's just
a "Mom."

Oh, no, it's
another "Mom."

It's just a
"Mom."

◎18◎

The Mom Card

People have often asked what the hardest part of being an Archery Mom is and at first I would have said it was coordinating all the travel. Then I would have said that it's balancing the highs and lows of three boys as they compete. Not many things are harder than having one son up in the clouds for a great tournament while another is down in the dumps from a substandard one. But then finally, I knew the hardest thing about being an archery mom was when someone played the "Mom Card."

I am not talking about the Mom Card that gets played by moms themselves, the classic, "You'll do as I say because I am the Mom!" I am talking about the other "Mom Card." This Mom Card is delivered by those who can't adjust to the fact that a parent can indeed successfully coach their own children, albeit we test each other many times. This Mom Card gets played by judges who are arrogant or by others who want to diminish the hard work that parents put into the job of helping our kids succeed, whether it's in archery or in some other endeavor. At one event there was discussion as to whether I was "allowed" to stand behind Dakota during elimination matches because according to one @$&#! Judge I was "Just a Mom." This was not met with happiness by my sons.

I had never dealt with the Mom Card being played on

111

me because we hadn't participated in competition sports before, but I quickly realized what it was and why it got played. "You're just the Mom" and "Oh, you're his mother" were comments thrown out when I would do what other coaches who were not related to an archer would do to stand up for their archers or work through an issue for their archers. I not only learned to coach, to be a bow mechanic, to seek information when I needed/wanted it, but also I poured my heart into becoming the best coach I could be and at the same time do what many coaches will not do . . . because I am their mom.

Excuse . . . me.

I attended the same trainings as every other person who has become a certified Archery Coach. In fact, I attended extra training courses because I coached a high level athlete; so when I achieved the title of Regional Coach in 2007 I had paid out of pocket more than most people to attend coach certification courses. I write letters to the USA Archery Board not because I am a mom but because I want to protect the rights of all athletes, and I think all coaches should write letters when things are screwy. I don't have to go to tournaments, but I think the boys are entitled to have their coach present and, apparently, so do they. I'm entitled to stand behind my sons in matches and I'm entitled to everything else every other coach is entitled to, despite the Mom Card being thrown out there as if it were a Cardinal Sin to coach your own children.

There are many benefits to having your coach be your mom (or dad). One of the things my sons never had to think about was, "Will she go to bat for us when there is an issue on the field?" Nor did they have to wonder if their coach would show up. Nor did they have to worry if they could afford a coach. Well, they did have to worry about that because I was also smart enough to know that I didn't know it all (not even close to all). But that's a different story.

It's not easy coaching your own, as many of us who do have discovered. It's a delicate balancing act to know when you are pushing enough, when you have pushed too far, when you ought to just get in the car and scream to yourself, when you need a glass of wine or maybe two (after every single tournament!), when you need to ask for help and when to turn them over to someone else. And sometimes through this wild adventure of being an Archery Mom, I have lost that balance. And gratefully, my sons usually let me know when. And those who care about us have as well. Nothing is more sobering than having a 16-year old putting his arm around you saying, "Mom, calm down" just as you are about to throttle someone for being a blithering idiot. And there are times that my sons have thanked me for exactly being the "Mom Who Coaches Them" in spite of the times that I fell off that balance bar that we all needed to be on to succeed.

I fully acknowledge that we started out in this sport choosing a first bow with the brilliant question, "Clarke, do you want the long curvy one or the one with wheels?" and in less than three years from their very first lesson we had National Champions, World Team members, All-Americans, All-Academic Archery Team members, U.S. Archery Team members, and more. We have learned tricks, tips, and basic know-how from some of the best coaches and archers in the U.S. But ask my boys who is their coach and they'll say "My mom." Why, after all the great people we've worked with would they say that? Because Mom is always there. She'll be there when no one else is available. Always. I had to learn to deal with the Mom Card being played and so did the boys.

Yep, I'm a mom. And sometimes that's the best thing in the world to be. I have told the boys many times, "No one in the world will stick up for you, or help you, or watch out for you, or stand by you like your mom will." Such is the case for the Sinclair Boys, so when other people make the comment, "She's only a mom" I finally figured they must be saying that because they know those truths. I am their mom . . . and coach . . . and chauffeur . . . and travel agent . . . and cook . . . and whatever else it takes to help them reach their goals. It works for us and that's all that counts.

Dakota with the team from Trinidad and Tobago

◎19◎

Dislocated in the Dominican Republic

"Mom, open the door, I'm hurt."

In our first venture together outside the country, Dakota and I had flown down to the World Ranking Event in the Dominican Republic by ourselves. Neither of us spoke Spanish and I had the typical worrier mom thoughts, "What if something should happen? We don't even speak the language!" Everyone says I worry too much . . . but. The boys had pulled many pranks on me over the years "my shoulder is hurt, my arm is hurt, I'm hurt . . . ha, ha, ha. . . . you always fall for it, Mom."

I sat outside at the field in the heat and humidity all day while Dakota practiced and now I'm in the shower trying to wash off the day's sweat. We were going to go to a shopping mall with the archers from Trinidad, Tobago, and Barbados whom we had befriended the first few days. After an impressive practice, Dakota had headed to the pool to cool off. As I'm showering I heard, "Mom, I'm hurt." Thinking that he was pulling a prank, I yelled that I would be out in a minute, he kicked the door and yelled, "No, Mom, I'm hurt for real. You need to open the door."

117

The voice had changed from the first request and panic hit me as I shut off the water and grabbed a towel. His voice was filled with pain and he kicked the door again, "Mom!"

I hurried as fast as I could to pull some clothes on and opened the door—to see Dakota's right arm dangling out of its socket. It's hard to explain what that looks like exactly other than distorted, ugly, and scary. Dripping wet and barely dressed I pounded on the door next to us, that of our friends from Trinidad and talked as fast as I could when the door opened.

Our room quickly filled with archers from Trinidad, Tobago, and other countries as well as coaches from Chile, Mexico, Venezuela and a few others. I could hear snippets of conversation about "the American who shot so well at practice" and about the "Americano." Everyone was concerned and trying to decide what needed to be done, what could be done. Should we take him to a local hospital? Or get on a plane to the U.S. or even to California? Should we try to set it ourselves? All these questions were swirling around the room in a mixture of English, Spanish, and other languages. It was amazing how much support and information was passing through the room. I had heard of the phrase "it takes a village," but I rapidly learned what that meant in the global community of archery. Such kindness from total strangers was incredible. One Coach who had set partial dislocations before told me it was too serious of an injury for us to resolve. He said Dakota needed professional medical care. Hmmm, okay. Here or the United States? More discussion . . . and more discussion . . . then a decision. It would be here in the Dominican Republic. Okay, how the heck do we do that?

From the moment the decision was made to get medical help things moved rapidly without my even having to ask. One person talked to the front desk and arranged for a cab; someone else called the local hospital to make sure they would be able to help us. Our friend George Vire from the Trinidad & Tobago team began throwing my stuff into his fanny pack and grabbed some of his own money "just in case." We had no idea what to expect, but as we left our room escorted by several kind strangers, I was reassured over and over in broken English, "No worry, mamá, he'll be alright."

"No worry, mamá, he'll be alright."

George, Dakota, and I piled into the taxicab where George took over the logistics. I wasn't able to think. What no one knew (and I wasn't about to say) was that I was struggling with a great many emotions. I felt frozen. I still was dealing with post traumatic stress from Clarke's accident. I wasn't prepared for Dakota to be seriously injured.

Archery is where we had put our energy from the time the boys made the decision they wanted to compete; where we had put our energy when we lost Clarke; where Dakota had put his energy to excel, having taken a year off of school to train fulltime, first at the Olympic Training Center and then on his own. I knew he was thinking the same things I was: "What now?" and "Will I be able to shoot again?" All the same questions rolling around in our heads and I had no answers. I couldn't even ask the taxi driver how much longer it would take as Dakota recoiled in pain at every bump in the road and corner we turned. I certainly could hardly start sorting out what had just happened and what it would mean

119

down the road.

Arriving at the hospital, we were overcome with emotions, while the taxi driver just wanted us to get out and pay him. The hesitation was that the building the taxi driver is assuring us is a hospital doesn't look anything like a medical facility. It actually looks like an old, make that a really old, house. George tells us that the taxi driver is certain it is indeed the "médica." We gingerly got Dakota out of the taxi and went inside.

"Does anyone speak English?" I'm worried . . . the room is a combined check-in area, emergency room, and waiting room. The only separation is some curtains that block off the sides of the portion designated as the emergency room. Surrounded by chaos, we are met with blank looks, stares, and curiosity. I'm handed paperwork in Spanish. A baby, getting oxygen and turning blue, is screaming as his mother holds him right next to the check-in desk. Another man is wheeled in as his tearful family follows. He looks ashen and unconscious. Behind a curtain a few feet away someone's child is shrieking and Dakota is trying to bolt for the door: "I'm not staying here!" I'm thinking to myself and I may have even said it aloud, "Uh, yes you are, we don't have any other choice." We show the woman at the desk the dangling arm and her face reflects that she understands we have an emergency. She takes us to one of the beds that have curtains on either side. Dakota is reeling from all the screaming and chaos in the "médica," plus the pain is increasing.

Finally, I get my wits about me and start asking questions with George's help. Is there a doctor? Does anyone speak English? We need to find someone to help us. And then Dakota says, "Yeah and I need to make sure they don't give me anything that wouldn't pass anti-doping rules for USADA." Oh geez, really? I thought, who would've thought about that one in the middle of all of this? Okay, so add to the list, no drugs unless we know what it is. How will I translate the drug name into English? How will I check to make sure it's an acceptable drug? Really? I have to address this, yep, because now Dakota emphatically declares, "They aren't giving me anything! Nothing!"

Heck, I'm not even sure they will help us. We aren't from their country. Do they accept Blue Cross in the Dominican Republic? I dunno and I look at George, who is amazing and talking to Dakota in an attempt to distract him. I think he was telling jokes at one point, but I can't honestly remember. It seemed so surreal.

A nurse arrives with needles and Dakota goes off the chart again about USADA. So now we are trying to explain that we need to know what they are trying to give him so we can "approve" it. After a lot of back and forth, with pigeon Spanish and George's help, we finally hit on the right words Archery (mimic shooting) and Olímpico. We are nodding our heads, Yeah, you got it . . . wants to go to the Olimpiadas. We need to make sure he doesn't get drugs that would get him banned from competition. What a magic word Olímpico was. The relief on the nurse's face was very apparent when she realized that we weren't trying to keep him from getting help, we just needed to know what they were trying to do.

"Okay, okay" the nurse tells us, and she takes off with-out further words. She's back very quickly with Dr. Pietro in tow; she points to Dakota and mimics archery and says the magic words again, "Olímpico" and more words fol-low (which we later learn she was telling him that Dakota aspires to be an Olympian and they needed to take good care of him). "Ohhh. . . ," Dr. Pietro murmurs, "Olímpico, Archery. I like archery."

"No worry mamá, he'll be okay."

That's the assurance of Dr. Pietro. Somehow I believe him. And George sits smiling as finally we have help and understanding of what we have been trying to say for an hour.

The drugs, finally administered, lessen the pain and make Dakota talk even more rapidly. It's funny since most of what he says makes no sense and he is usually so logical. But what does make sense is when the Doctor returns and tells us that first we need to do X-Rays and then surgery. Dakota tries to get up off the table as he vigorously proclaims, "No surgery!' as George, Dr. Pietro and I block the exit. And then I know what he's afraid of, because I'm afraid of it myself and he quietly whispers to me, "Mom, I don't want them to put me under (anesthesia)."

Yep, we think alike, we have the same fears and I'm not sure what to do so I ask Dr. Pietro if we can keep him awake. I'm told absolutely not (well, George translated that for me). Somewhere in the two hours that have passed, Barbara Hernandez from the Dominican Archery Organization shows up to help. We were so relieved to have someone who could speak both English and Spanish, even though with George's help we had stumbled through the past two hours and had a good understanding of what needed to be done. And I had filled out the paperwork, I think correctly. (I could figure out enough of the form.) What I still didn't know is how to pay for it or how much it would cost. George assured me he would give us all the cash he had and we would find an ATM to get more if we needed it. Barbara took charge of that entire situation and worked with the hospital staff making arrangements and finally telling me, "the operation will cost $600. My organization will pay for it and you can reimburse us later." I'm from America, okay, where healthcare is expensive and $600 might pay for a band aid and an aspirin. So I ask, "$600? What does that cover: sitting on the bed and the exam?" No, it covers everything she assures me. All I had to do was agree to re-pay it later. Okay, I can do that. Dakota repeats incredulously, "$600 is all they want? What can they do for $600?" Okay, so maybe it wasn't good that Barbara could speak English and he could overhear everything we were saying because there was no place for private conversations. While discussing all this we were standing outside the curtains like he couldn't hear us. Sheesh!

Barbara finishes making the financial arrangements and stays with us a little while longer. Eventually she has to get back to running a World Ranking Event and she tells us she will see us back at the hotel. A nurse comes and tries to explain it is time for the X-Rays and we are summoned to follow. They tell George to wait, but they let me go in with Dakota. We enter a room that is the size of a small walk-in closet with a doorway to a larger walk-in closet. I figured out (hey, I'm thinking fast by this time) that the first room is where the person stands when taking the X-Ray and the larger closet has the X-Ray machine and the patient. Trouble is the X-Ray machine looks ancient. Really ancient, maybe even a first edition. And this is noticed by my son who hasn't stopped talking since the second round of pain meds. Dakota looks at me with a cocked eyebrow and says, "I don't think that I need an X-Ray; otherwise you can forget about grandchildren." Okay, well, mother and son have another tête à tête and I explain they need to take the X-Rays with that machine. I explain that I do understand and agree that he will probably glow in the dark later, and yes it does appear that it might be one of the original X-Ray machines, but we're doing it anyways. So it's no surprise when they shuttle him into the larger room (as I had surmised was for the patient and the machine). But it was a big surprise when they say, "Mamá, you come too. We need you to help." Me? Really? Okay. . . .

"Hold arm in this position." Mostly we communicate by miming, but I get it and if I mimed this it would be a little hard for you to read. I get it . . . hold his arm . . . okay, "Hey, why are you leaving! Wait a second," Brrrt, Click. X-ray taken. The man re-enters the room and moves the arm into a new position and gestures for me to hold it. "Okay, but, um, can we talk for a minute?" Apparently not as he moves quickly out of the room as if I'm not talking at all and Brrrt, Click. X-ray taken again.

"Um, Mom?" Yes, Dakota? "Um, you definitely can forget about grandchildren. There's no lead protection on any part of us and, ummm, don't you think it's weird they left you in here?" We're the family that does everything possible to minimize X-Rays. We've just been nuked and we know it.

We leave the X-Ray room and are escorted to an elevator. Dakota takes one look at it and suggests plummeting to the basement really isn't the best plan. He wants to walk to wherever we are going. No one understands us, so it doesn't really matter that we aren't comfortable. They hold the elevator door and, smiling, gently nudge my son inside, along with another medical worker, a man on a gurney, and the person taking us to the "operación." I am glad George is still with us so I am not alone and Dakota just wants to flat out leave. He keeps talking about how we could get a plane to the U.S. and get the arm fixed. I remind him that I have his dad working on getting us out of the country, but I have no idea how that is working out and we have to get the arm set before we can leave. He's not happy, so they inject him with some more drugs.

The creaking elevator opens up on another floor and another nurse's station. Dakota is so overly aware now that he notices the large bug walking across the floor and the missing tiles. I try to distract him with how his dad is going to get us home and George talks to him as well. Finally Dr. Pietro comes out and as I start to stand up to go with Dakota, he says, "No, mamá, you cannot come. It is time for operación." Reluctantly, I watch as Dr. Pietro and Dakota disappear behind the doors. George reassures me that everything is going to be alright. Deep breath! Another deep breath. Okay, lots of deep breaths.

About 15 minutes later, Dr. Pietro returns and my heart leaps in panic. How could he be done already?

"Mamá, you can come back here." What? Already?' Uhhh . . . as it is explained to me on the way back into the operating area, my son won't let them put him under the anesthesia and has done everything possible to keep that from happening. So "mamá" is being brought in to get him to cooperate. Oh good, I have some use after all.

It took some talking and explaining that the man laying on the gurney next to Dakota's bed was not dead. He had the blanket over his face because he was cold and still waiting for his surgery. It took more talking to answer his questions and yes, I was afraid he might die, but we had to do it anyway. Slowly, the anesthesia took effect and I returned to the waiting area.

"Mamá, you can come back again. He won't stop talking about seeing his mom." The drugs had really kicked in and Dr. Pietro said Dakota was very talkative. This time I was greeted with a smile and assurances that his arm felt great, how much he loved me, and that it was time to return to the USA. It all sounded good to me.

We returned to the motel and found out we couldn't leave until the next morning. Our friends from Trinidad and Barbados helped make sure we had ice. (That's a lot more work than you can imagine as they only gave out ice in the drinks, not for ice packs.) They helped me get everything packed. We got up early the next morning as everyone else was getting on the buses to go to the field for the qualification round. Dakota and I hugged all our new friends good bye and got into a taxi to the airport.

Stateside, the shoulder surgeon told us that Dr. Pietro had done a fantastic job setting the shoulder and that Dakota could go back to shooting in a short time. About twelve weeks after the dislocation, he placed fourth at the World Target Trials, missing a spot on the team by one quarter of a point. While we were assured the shoulder was solid, there were some ongoing issues that resulted in another injury at the Texas Shootout in 2009. Dakota had surgery in June 2009 and was back shooting his bow the following March. It's hard to understand how much work he put into his recovery. He never let up and continues to practice six days a week while maintaining honors as a fulltime student at UC San Diego.

"No worry mamá, he'll be . . ."

It takes a village—even in the world of archery. The concern, compassion, assurances, and well-wishes in multiple languages by archers and coaches from all over the world reminded me why we had embraced archery when our sons fell in love with the sport. There are many people who were at the tournament in the Dominican Republic who helped us whose names I do not know, but wish to thank for their offer of friendship and support. The language of archery is universal and it certainly showed for two Americans far from home.

A special thanks to Jonathan Kacal, George, the rest of the Trinidad and Tobago Team, Shane DeFreitas from Barbados, and Barbara Hernandez from the Dominican Republic. If it wasn't for your friendship and support, that miserable accident would have been a hundred times worse. George, you were my hero that day and I can't thank you enough for being there for Dakota and me.

◎ 20 ◎

Finding the F-U-N in Archery Again

What started out as a birthday present on April 1, 2002, in complete innocence and with complete ignorance of what archery was about, what once was nothing more than excitement and entertainment, what once was an opportunity to learn something new, an opportunity to excel at a sport, slowly and surely wound its way—sometimes meandering, sometimes plowing headlong, but always with us unsuspecting and not realizing—into becoming a sort of monster into which we temporarily lost ourselves.

In 2005, our family poured it's heart and soul into archery. At that time it was a necessity—it was survival—it's all we knew how to do in order to survive the loss of my son, Clarke. Archery gave us a home, if for no other reason than it occupied us, kept us busy, and gave our minds somewhere to focus our attention so that each miserable day that passed gave us some other thoughts besides those on whom we lost. Losing your son is forever, so it's not like I woke up one day and the world was wonderful again, but time does help you move forward. I have often said that archery saved us those first few years, and gave my sons somewhere to go, something to work towards, and overall gave our family a "home" that we desperately needed. I didn't intend for it to lose its appeal or become something we would loathe more than love.

What began as "something to do" turned into dreams and aspirations and goals. Being at the top, making Olympic teams, making World Championship teams, those are not bad things to achieve or to strive for. Most people spend some time and effort to be good at something, whatever brings them joy and pleasure. We were slightly different in that we were also struggling to live as well. As the boys practiced and competed and did the training required to become top athletes, their skills improved and, without realizing what was going on, they began to make progress that was as rapid as it was unexpected. It was exciting at the time. Dakota's first National Indoor Championship was the first of those successes. We thought we were doing well; we also thought we knew what we were doing. The achievements became important validations that what we were doing was correct and promising, and motivating . . . so we pushed harder and set more goals and made more plans. I use the word "we" because behind every great archer there is a "team" of unflagging support, a team of people who, no matter what, win or lose, sink or swim, won't abandon you. And the core of that team, as it turns out, was the remaining four people in our family. While other people came and went from our "team," the four of us stood together, as we always had when we were a team of five.

In the midst of working towards membership on a U.S. Archery Team (USAT) and rising in the "rolling rankings," training full-time, going to school full-time, working part-time, competing locally, regionally, nationally . . . and making ends meet courtesy of our Visa card and savings, silently cringing every time someone said, "Mom, I need. . . ," knowing that a few more hundred dol-

lars were about to go to an equipment company, it began to feel, at least some days, like a "grind."

The advancement of your athlete up the ranks might turn out different from what you think; that's my experience anyways. Expectations rise with the advancement, not just for yourself and your athlete, but of their coach, their friends, and others in the sport of archery. People start paying attention and with that there are new pressures, new issues, and the world morphs some more. But you are unaware of this because your experiences don't include the myriad things that are a part of being a top athlete or his support crew. You find your friends change, your kid's friends change, your kids change, and without the experience of "I have been here before," you have no idea what is going on or why. There is a sudden push that at first felt like momentum but in retrospect felt like a kick in various parts of my body, and I'm not even the one training and competing, I'm just the sponsor and bus driver!

People you thought you knew, you didn't. People you trusted, you shouldn't have. People you don't know at all, save you by being kind, only to discover that they've been where you are, so they know what you are learning. And you discover that things are not what you thought and archery is more complex than you ever imagined and, yes, there are politics—even in archery! Maybe "especially" in archery, because it's such a small sport, and like Alice in Wonderland, you feel like you fell down the rabbit hole and are dazed and confused . . . and you are too young to have lived through the 60's so you don't recognize the full experience of dazed and confused, but you know that something isn't right. Sitting down in the rabbit hole, not knowing which road to take, which way to turn, the only thing you know is that your kids are good at something and that you used to enjoy it, but somewhere in the last few years, you and they have lost that thrill, that moment of excitement, and you know that something is wrong and things must change.

The thrill of being "ranked," the thought of receiving a supporting stipend, the idea of having priority to attend international tournaments—yeah, it sounded good . . . and necessary. And we were convinced that we had to go to every national tournament, we had to spend every last dollar we had available, we had to make sure that training stayed at six days a week, we had to maintain cardiovascular and strength training no matter what, that we had to track scores, practice, acquire coaching, do extra training and we had to do whatever we could so that we could . . . we could . . . uhh . . . we could one day wake up and think, "I don't love archery so much anymore."

Yes, that's what happened one morning—well, okay two, three, sixteen, forty mornings in a row—and I couldn't quite figure it out. I love archery . . . I do . . . so why did I wake up with "I don't love archery so much anymore" rolling around in my head day after day? Why was I cringing at the thought of going to tournaments, of buying equipment, of passing on a Hawaiian vacation so that the boys could go to an "important" event instead, an event not even in a vacation spot, rather a windy place or a rainy place or a humid place, and not even on premiere fields, fields that I thought premiere tournaments would be held on. No, we end up on dirt for days, with sand and grit blowing all over us or standing on a hillside on a south facing field with sun blaring in the face of the left-handed boy or in a major international team trial with freezing temperatures and wind and rain all because someone somewhere decided it just had to be at a location that didn't make any sense for that time of year. And I'm paying for all of this because my sons are good at something and we need to do everything we can to make sure they do well. What could possibly make me loathe archery, when my sons were national champions, ranked in the top 10 of their divisions and working towards "being ranked" and getting "stipends" and "benefits" and "special coaching" and "international competition opportunities" . . . what the heck was going on?

Oh. . . !

It took days, weeks really, to fully pinpoint what was bugging me; it took sitting down and really thinking it through . . . and seeing how the priorities had blurred, gotten skewed—not without help, mind you—from the subtle and sometimes not so subtle pressures to "advance," to "do better," to "be at the top," or to "make a team," because if you didn't, the world will . . . the world will . . . uhh. . . ah, the world will just keep on going. As it so happened, one son missed the World Target Team by ¼ of a ranking point. Yes, the sun was still yellow the next day, the sky was still blue, and the stipend was still going to someone else—and the Visa card still had a balance—and the young man was still talented in archery, but he wasn't having fun anymore either . . . and that worried me. We weren't having fun and life experience has taught me that life is short. Life should be fun and anyone's expectations, even mine, should not change that.

It was an epiphany—a good thing, because boy did I need one—for all of us. Because another truism that I know is that where The Mom dwells, so does the family . . . and I was dwelling in the pits . . . the darkness . . . buried deep underneath the expectations of things that truly do not matter in the grand scheme of things.

Basically, I lost the F in fun, and then I lost the U, and then the N. And I found other adjectives, not very happy ones, replacing what were once the simple thrills from just a few years ago, of seeing the smile on my sons' faces when they hit the paper, never mind the yellow.

Sitting on the sofa, meditation tapes blaring, I understood what had happened. I knew what had to be done, I just wasn't sure how to do it. How to go backward, how to not care about ranking, about top finishes, about sponsorships, about stipends, about what the High Performance Committee thought of my sons, of what other people's expectations were, of what other people would say . . . when and if we dared to practice two days a week instead of six, to let cardio slide because they literally hate it, to not compete at certain events because the fields were miserable and the tournament wasn't fun. I found that I wasn't only stuck with my expectations, I was stuck with other people's as well and I wasn't even the one shooting and competing; I'm the sponsor and bus driver!

As I rolled these thoughts around in my Buddha-consciousness, I could only imagine what my sons' pressures were (they absorb everything) and I already knew that they too had lost the F-U-N. I knew it because, well, we talk and they had said so.

The "idea" of going backward is easier said than done, but that became the goal and it's hard work and a grind of a different kind because you have to change your mindset; you have to set aside not only your own expectations, but your sons' also, and especially the expectations and attitudes of others. And you have to learn to look with innocence again . . . at those skinny sticks and that target far, far away and learn to marvel at the amazing beauty of those sticks being loosed from the string and flying to the target to end up in the yellow . . . at how amazing that once seemed, and finding that "thrill" has to become the focus again.

Or we were on fast track to burnout, sure as shooting.

Flash forward a few months and we are at the Collegiate nationals, where at first things were not going well due to outside influences and then we, as a family, remembered our goals: to find the F in the fun and with our decision to escape the "whatevers" of others; I once again watched with joy as my son not only won the team trial but then smiling turned and yelled, "Mom! Will you coach me through the Olympic Rounds?" For the first time in a long time, the fun was creeping back into our lives through archery and it was something we wanted to hang on to. It was a chance to move backward and rekindle the love of simply "hitting the paper."

And though there were moments of frustration during the week, our determination to do what was right by our family, for ourselves, to find not only the F but the U and the N again, caused the negative moments, pushed by others, to matter for naught, because their issues belong only to them; they don't live my life, they don't walk in my shoes. And they aren't my family, who loves to shoot archery, for the fun of it.

We talked and laughed through the early matches. We found the "sync" that we had had long before we let others take over the relationship that once was only ours and found ourselves, as a team of mother/coach and son/athlete, in the gold medal match, meeting a goal with ease and without thought. The final arrow of the OR match was a 10, there was no way to lose the championship and it felt like a slow-motion moment from long ago, a reflection of 2004 when Clarke made the Jr. World Team and I found him hugging me tightly with a grin that wouldn't go away, except this time it was Dakota, and the smile on his face, displaying the notion that he had not only won but he had had *fun* doing it, and winning once again was the icing on the cake, not the focus of our attention.

It's been a long road, and it is a continuing process. Walking backwards, not caring about stipends, not caring about the U.S. Archery Team or rolling rankings, not caring about invitations for special coaching, not worrying about placing in the top three at a tournament or making a team and definitely not worrying about what other people think, but rather just shooting because the feel of cleanly loosing an arrow is something that few people actually get to do in the world and knowing that feeling, that essence of the arrow flying 200 feet per second towards a piece of paper and landing in the 10 ring, that feeling of success, for the intrinsic value of that, that's what archery used to be about for us and that's what we strive for it to be again.

◎ 21 ◎

Aged Out
(The Boys Grow Up)

We started archery when Barrett was 10, Clarke 13, and Dakota 16. In 2009 Barrett turned 18 and "aged out" of the JOAD program. I'm glad. It's been a long eight years, sometimes happy, sometimes not, but I'm looking forward to new endeavors. I'll always be an Archery Mom, but I won't always have to be the one who coordinates all the practices, training, tournaments, and coaching. It's their turn to take part of the duties and make archery whatever it's going to be for them in their lives.

Barrett sort of burned out on JOAD over the last few years. Now that he's a full-time college student, he has the option of moving into a college program or shooting Senior division with the big guns or being a recreational shooter while he works towards his degree(s) in psychology and business. Whether he shoots in college, or not, doesn't matter to me. What matters is that he shoots for himself.

Dakota has been in the college program for four years, winning the national title four times, earning All-American and All-Academic honors all four years, and has made four world teams. While he has been in and out of school, in and out of full-time training, undergoing shoulder surgery, ordinary life events, and whatever else

139

has put him on the "six years to a bachelor's degree" track, the one constant has been archery. He loves it and I am happy. I hope he is still shooting in 50 years like our friend Ed Eliason. I hope he finds joy and happiness from the sport for a very long time. I don't care if he becomes an Olympian, I don't care if he wins a gold medal. I don't even care if he competes. I only hope that he always looses that feeling when he looses an arrow and it flies towards the gold and hits with a mighty "thwack!" That sound, I love that sound. It is what first hooked me on archery . . . well, that and the smile on my three sons' faces the first time Larry Smith told them, "Just open your hand and let it go." That moment is with me forever as are all the moments of joy and sadness that we have had since then – the tournament stress, the wins, the losses, the traveling, the politics, the wondering how we were going to pay for it all. Nothing subsequent was better than that first time they let an arrow fly.

The moments I most loved with my sons and being an Archery Mom:

- Dakota winning the US Intercollegiate Archery Championships (USIACs) in 2008. His smile as he nailed the 10-ring with his last arrow and knew he had won and the huge hug he gave me, bow still attached to his hand, as he scooped me up and said, "Thanks, Mom" and then went to call his dad.
- Barrett winning the U.S. Target Outdoor Championship in 2007. Seeing Barrett coming into his own (which was something Mike Gerard had commented on in 2004, that Barrett needed "to figure out his place in all of this with two older brothers who were so passionate about, and good at, archery"). Seeing Barrett do exactly that—finding his stride—was better than actually winning . . .

well, to me it was. I'm sure Barrett found 1st place to be the "best."

- February 2007. Dakota deciding that he would stay true to himself and train the way he felt was best for him. (And he continues to do so with his dad working with him since 2009.)
- September 7, 2004. Watching Clarke and Barrett walking to the target at our house, Clarke's arm draped over his little brother, and shouting out to me with a huge smile on his face, "Hey Mom! He just shot a 56 at 50 meters!" and then leaning into Barrett and saying, "You're going to be even better than me someday." It was almost prophetic as Clarke died the next day.
- All the times the Cache Valley crew came to our house to shoot and we laughed and barbequed.
- Clarke making the Jr. World Team in 2004. That day we saw the payoff of his determination. The months of hard work standing in the spring snow, freezing while he and Dakota shot in hail, wind, and rain as they prepared to try out for the team, Clarke always saying, "I'm going to make this team." And when he did make the team—the smile on his face as he walked off the line and gave Mike Gerard a huge hug and told Larry Smith "thank you" were defining moments of my shy son Clarke, who always knew it was a team effort.
- Spring Classic, April 2004, Mission Viejo, CA. The boys and I drove from Utah to California in one day. It was a 14 hour drive, with only two stops, so they could shoot in the Spring Classic held by the Saddleback Archery Club. All three boys returned with medals (and new friends: the Holstein kids, the Reiss kids) and Saddleback Archery became part of our lives. Clarke and Dakota had a shoot-off for the bronze medal in a Combined

Olympic Round—my first time watching my sons compete against one another. This wasn't something I looked forward to but it turned out, it was my last time as well, so I have no idea how I would have handled it later. (I hope like most good Archery Moms . . . with grace.) Katie Reiss and Gary Holstein both reached out to me when we lost Clarke five months later, and sadly, my turn came to reach out to Katie in 2008 when her son was killed in a motorcycle accident.

- The Las Vegas Shoot, February 2004. The birthplace of the Archery Mafia (Chris, Paul, Me, Dakota, and Clarke). Barrett joined the Mafia in September 2004 and Bob in December 2004)
- April 1, 2002. The boy's first archery lesson at Salt Lake Archery, and not coincidentally Clarke's 13th birthday. Larry, like all good coaches, hooked them on the first arrow and had the entire family in love with archery within a short time afterwards.

The people who most impacted our archery lives:
- Larry Smith, owner of Salt Lake Archery, the boys' first coach and our friend forever.
- The Cache Valley Archers: Mike Beeny, Herb Mays, Lynn Mays, Claudia Beeny, Riley Whiting, Pat Christensen, and Leslie Bush. They made archery fun.
- Ed Eliason, "Life Lessons from Ed" will always be a part of our conversation whether it involves archery or just "life."
- Mike Gerard, one of the nicest people in the world and the best teacher for equipment we have ever come across.
- The Cache Valley JOAD Program, all the kids that were part of the program when Mike, Herb, and I started the club in the fall of 2004.

- Leslie Howa, because she's Leslie.
- Bob Romero, who taught us so much.

I got involved in College Archery in 2005 and have held many positions at the same time as being a full-fledged Archery Mom. I became the Director in 2009 and began opening the doors to more archers by being inclusive no matter what type of bow one shot, no matter what "game" you played (3-D, field, target, etc.). I believe in that.

Coming from Logan, Utah, where my sons were the only recurve archers in the valley, we hung out with the compound archers of Cache Valley and we learned a lot and made good friends. Many times, the "adults" would get onto me about the boys competing against compound archers, feeling the boys should get handicapped, and I would always say, "There will be no giving them points because they're going to get so good, they'll beat you straight up." And they did, because my sons always rise to a challenge, no matter what it is. And that is one of the most important things archery has given us: it showed us that even in the face of tragedy, we could push ourselves to dream, to believe, and to achieve.

◎ 22 ◎

Random Things I Have Learned as an Archery Mom

Everyone wants their kid to win.

There're politics in everything – really!

The more successful your kids are,
the more you recognize the politics.

You gotta do the "right thing"
whether your family benefits or not.

You gotta do the "hard thing"
even if it makes people mad at you.

Practice really does improve shooting.

Tournament stress is underrated.

Tournament wins are overrated.

It's a game—really—involving skinny sticks
flying through the air to a target.

It's supposed to be fun . . .

. . . and if it's not, then you might rethink that.

You won't make a million dollars in archery,
no matter how successful you are.

Setting goals is important—unless it
defines your success and failure.

Archery is a part of life, not life itself.

You should always be polite.

Watch for the parents who are new—they are usually
suffering from *archeryitis*—give them a break,
they'll learn.

Offer your shade to strangers—they will become your
friends, especially if they are from Canada.

Take a sock to a tournament—when you are really frustrated with some blathering off the wall parent who
doesn't "get it," look at the sock and remember how you,
too, needed to "stuff it," probably not all that long ago.

Success is not measured by getting on a special team,
winning a tournament, or getting sponsored.

Success is measured by who you are as a person—
and how you handle yourself as
an Archery Mom (or Archery Dad).

Bring rain gear—no matter what
the weather report says—'cuz they lie!

When you see a kid who needs sunblock,
remember: all kids belong to you at an archery
tournament when it comes to
water, food, and sunblock.

Be nice to the judges—they don't get paid
and their job is hard.

Tell the judge to respect your kids—they have
the same rights as any other archer on the field!

Pull out your equipment box and help repair
someone's equipment. It either will come in
handy for you down the road or you will
always know you weren't afraid to
help a competitor—either way you win.

Duct tape really is one of the wonders of the world.
Make it a "must have" item in your travel kit.

Make sure your kids shake hands with their
competitors—it's the right thing to do.

If you are good, you don't need to let everyone know; they
already know and you will just look foolish or arrogant.

Clarke Sinclair Memorial
Archery Scholarship

www.clarkesinclair.org

Clarke's Scholarship was established to honor Clarke Robert Sinclair (April 1989–Sept 2004). Clarke was a Cadet recurve archer who not only loved the sport, but also achieved a great deal in a very short time. From the day of his first archery lesson on April 1, 2002 until the day he died, Clarke gave 100% all the time. His goals and dreams were to make more world teams and someday represent the US at the Olympics. His achievements of ranking #4 in the U.S. and making the 2004 Jr. World Team in two years from his first exposure to archery were remarkable. His dedication made us proud and our family wanted to honor Clarke's commitment by supporting other youth and collegiate archers. From our own experience, we know how difficult and expensive it is to fund elite archers to important competitions.

And we believe in dreams . . .

CSMAS supports youth and collegiate archers who are good role models, outstanding archers, and who work hard, like Clarke did, to achieve their goals.

CSMAS is dedicated to the promotion of competition in elite amateur archery. We provide charitable support to youth and collegiate archers who do not receive funding from national associations or full funding from Universities.

To date, CSMAS has supported more than 50 youth and collegiate archers by providing scholarships ranging from $100 to $1000. The scholarships have been given to all levels of archers in order to support the dreams and aspirations of those who want to compete. From archers who started out by joining a college club to world Champions, we have had the honor and privilege of supporting this vital segment of archery in honor of Clarke.

Our dreams are bigger than this . . .

We would like to help promising archers who don't have access to coaching. We would like to be able to provide funding for backup equipment for those traveling to international events on behalf of the U.S. We would like to see an archer make a team, be handed the funding necessary to make their dreams a reality and let them be home practicing for the tournament instead of selling raffle tickets, putting up posters, or knocking on doors to secure assistance. We would like to see our elite youth and collegiate archers succeed at international tournaments. We would like to become a valuable resource to the archery community.

100% of all donations support youth and collegiate archers. Our family and Board of Directors pay for all overhead as well as serve as volunteers for the organization.

Donations are tax deductible. Clarke Sinclair Memorial Archery Scholarship is a non-profit 501(c)(3) corporation.

Donations can be made online at *www.clarkesinclair.org* or mailed to:

Clarke Sinclair
PO Box 1827
Ridgecrest, CA 93556

Support Clarke Sinclair Memorial Archery Scholarship and help fulfill the dreams of others who commit themselves to becoming elite archers.

About the Author
(What is She Up to Now?)

I always say that archery is like the *Hotel California*—you can check out, but you can never leave. I've tried. It doesn't work. Once you get archery in your veins, you might as well figure out *how* you're going to contribute because if you love it, you are an archer (or Archery Mom) for life.

I've been an Archery Mom and I still am and even though my role is less, my emotions are still the same. I expect the best from my sons in sportsmanship, in commitment, in giving it their best, whatever that best may be. I also expect the same from myself.

Both Dakota and Barrett are in college and focusing on what will provide them their futures: degrees in law and psychology. This gives my role as Archery Mom a different aspect. I now nag them more about studying than about practicing. Whew! At least we don't have to sit out in the heat, sand, rain, snow, or wind to do that!

Aside from my duties associated with being an Archery Mom to my three sons, namely becoming a certified Regional Coach, a bow equipment master, a travel agent, and the other many things that are required for the sport, I have been involved in College Archery since 2005. My first position was as the Publicist, a position created for me by my dear friend Bob Ryder who was then Director of College Archery. I had begged Bob (then a stranger) for something to do ("Let me help somehow," I begged.), to give me anything, just to help me fill my time to distract me from my grief from the loss of Clarke. He did that . . . and then some.

In my first year as Publicist, my husband Bob and I developed the College Archery website, then we gained sponsors for the All-America and All-Academic archers. We developed the All-America Poster and found money to fund its printing and distribution, including donations from Clarke's Scholarship, and we did everything we could think of to bring exposure to College Archery. We paid for much of it out of our own pockets. Our family budget had a line item for College Archery Expenses because, while the program was under the umbrella of the National Archery Association (*aka* USA Archery) College Archery didn't receive any funding at all. I poured my heart into Clarke's Scholarship and College Archery while trying to survive the pain of losing Clarke. It's no easy task and it's something that is day to day, never going away, but distractions do help.

The next year I was the Registrar, keeping track of eligibility of our college athletes along with being the Publicist and Webmaster (because no one else would take those roles). The next year I received a lovely and eloquent email from my dear friend Bob Ryder, extolling how wonderful I was . . . and that he was appointing me to be the Assistant Director, as well as being the Publicist, Webmaster, and Registrar (because no one else still would volunteer to take those roles). The next year, Bob's health necessitated he retire as Director and so, another email from Bob explaining that as Assistant Director I needed to assume that responsibility. Thank goodness I had already finagled other people to become the Webmaster and Publicist! And we convinced the fantastic Helen Sahi to be the Assistant Director! (And then we elected her to the USA Archery board which caused her to have to resign—what were we thinking? Oy, I digress.)

I took on the task of being USCA Director knowing there was, oh, so much to be done. What better place for me than College Archery, a program I believed in and that was filled with promise . . . albeit no money. Surrounded by hundreds of college students brimming with enthusiasm and fun, I took the helm of a program in serious decline and decided to do something about it.

Our first funding effort was a grant application I wrote to fully fund the 2008 World University Games Archery Team. I was told it would never happen, but someone believed in my dream and the Easton Sport Development Foundation awarded a grant and the first ever, fully-funded World University Team brought home medals from that championship in Taiwan. I was elated. Then I decided that if Mr. Easton believed that it was worth supporting, maybe he would help College Archery rebuild itself into the program it used to be, the one that birthed World Champions and Olympians and had clubs and teams throughout the U.S. So, I wrote another grant application and outlined the needs of our clubs, teams, and overall program. I wrote a business plan and set goals for College Archery. The grant was awarded and will fund the effort for three years.

In 2005 there were about 40 college clubs (reportedly there were about 300 in the heyday of the 70's and 80's). Today, we have 100 clubs on the roster, though many are small and fledgling. Rebuilding a program and making it inclusive for all college archers: Target, 3-D, Compound, Recurve, Traditional, Barebow, *Genesis*, Recreational and

Competitive (it doesn't matter to me as long as they get to shoot) is a time commitment similar to being an Archery Mom. In fact, it's exactly like being an Archery Mom, except it's with 500 archers and a lot more paperwork and phone calls. I still find myself at tournaments telling college archers to put on their sunscreen and get some water . . . and "Oh, please make sure you submit your eligibility paperwork!" and "Oh, by the way, I can help with. . . ." Yep, I'm an Archery Mom forever.

My College Archery duties now take me to garden spots such as Louisville, KY; Birmingham AL; Lansing, MI; and Steven's Point, WI. (Oh, why can't we do something in Hawaii for once?) Instead of dragging along shades and bow cases and tool boxes, on many of my trips I drag a laptop to do Power Point presentations regaling the virtues of College Archery. In between building the U.S. Collegiate Archery Association into an organization that the college students deserve, I drive to San Diego to see Dakota and volunteer as the coach of the UCSD archery team that Dakota started (and which garnered our very first All-America, Chris Luk, in 2010), and watching Barrett turn into a man before my very eyes, as I ramble on about how much work College Archery is, and what a commitment is involved, and how sick I am of being in motels (albeit I am now a Platinum Member of a motel chain), and he rolls his dark blue eyes and says, "What did you think would happen? You think you would leave archery? You're addicted."

I've dreamt that I went on a vacation that wasn't an archery tournament, where no bows were packed, no shade went through airport security, and I slept in and had a leisurely breakfast then I went sightseeing and experienced a lovely trip to somewhere wonderful. Then, I awoke in a sweat and realized I was in a motel—in Yankton, SD—and I tripped over the boys' bows as I went to the bathroom in the dark. There will be time for that vacation, some day.

❦

The US Collegiate Archery Association (USCA) is the next step for young archers who graduate from high school and go to college. USCA is an open and inclusive organization that provides opportunities for all college students to participate. Whether your goals are recreational or competition; and whether you enjoy 3-D or Target Archery, and no matter what type of bow you shoot: traditional, recurve, compound, Genesis, barebow or bowhunter, College Archery invites you to come and play.

The mission of the USCA is to serve as the governing body for both recreational and elite archery competition in college. Our Vision is to establish college archery as an integral part of the campus experience in as many colleges and universities as possible. The USCA works hard to ensure that beginning, intermediate and elite archers can enjoy the sport in college, and we strive to introduce archery to as many college students as possible.

USCA Competitions include state, regional and national championships, an opportunity to earn a spot on a World University Team and honors such as All-America, All-Academic, and National Champion titles.

For Students: If there isn't a club at the college of your choice, we will help students start one.

For Parents: To save someone's sanity—consider volunteering! We always need and welcome help!

To learn about College Archery visit
www.uscollegiatearchery.org

Archery Terminology for the Unfamiliar
or What the heck is she talking about?

ALL-AMERICAN COLLEGE ARCHER To achieve this award, an archer must meet specific scoring criteria and be ranked in the top ten in the compound or recurve division nationally.

ACADEMIC ALL-AMERICAN COLLEGIATE ARCHER To achieve this award, an archer must have scored in the top 25% in the Indoor Competition and hold a 3.0 or higher grade point average.

ARM GUARD Many archers wear a protective device on the inside of their forearm to protect it from being slapped by the bowstring.

ARROWS(*Jazz*, *ACE*, *X10*, Weak/Stiff) Arrows are made of tubes of stiff, low density material: wood, aluminum, carbon fiber, or a composite of carbon and aluminum tubing. They have a heavier point at one end and a nock, or notch, at the other. Near the nock, fletching is use to help stabilize the flight of the arrow. Arrows must be quite stiff, but crucially they must retain some ability to flex. Determining the correct degree of arrow stiffness is one of the keys to successful archery. Easton *ACE* and *X10* arrows are carbon wrapped aluminum tubes and are among the most popular arrows used by Olympic archers.

ARROW FLIGHT An arrow has a center of mass and a center of drag. The center of drag must be behind the center of mass and the further behind the better, otherwise the arrow will be unstable in flight.

ARROW POINTS Arrow points come in a variety of sizes and weights. Some are cemented onto or into the shaft, some are screwed into cemented in inserts. Having the arrow point heavier than any other comparable length of the arrow is crucial to good arrow flight. Points are made out of durable materials like steel to protect the arrow when, on occasion, something hard is hit.

BOW SIGHT On many bows a bow sight is attached to the riser on the side opposite from the arrow rest. Most target sights have an extension bar which places the sight's aperture out in front of the bow. The aperture is lined up with the desired hitting point of the arrow. Figuring out where to put the sight aperture for various targets is called "sighting in."

BOW TUNING Bow tuning is adjusting the bow and arrow to the archer's form and execution to achieve the best performance. To get the most from bow tuning the archer's shooting form and execution must be consistent. The main variables that effect bow performance for recurve bows are: draw weight/force, bowstring material and mass, brace height, arrow nocking point location and fit, position of the arrow rest, and pressure button pressure.

CLICKER A clicker is a device used to maintain the same draw length from shot to shot. Clickers are typically screwed or clamped to the bow and have an "arm" that slides along the arrow shaft when the arrow is drawn and falls off of the tip making an audible and tactile "click."

COMPOUND BOW A compound bow uses cams or eccentric wheels on the ends of the limbs to provide for a mechanical advantage drawing the bow. When at full draw, compound archers do not hold the entire weight/force of the draw on their fingers as in recurve archery. Typically only a small part (20-35%) of the draw force remains, giving compound archers more time at full draw to aim and execute the release of the shot.

COACH CERTIFICATION PROGRAMS To become a certified coach, individuals must complete a course or courses that range in length from a day to a week. USA Archery currently has five levels of coach certification that can be earned.

CSMAS The Clarke Sinclair Memorial Archery Scholarship is provided by a non-profit foundation created to honor Clarke Sinclair through the awarding of scholarships to elite youth and collegiate archers.

DRAW LENGTH Draw Length is the distance from the bow string at the nocking point to the arrow rest hole plus 1¾" when the bow is at full draw.

DRAW WEIGHT Draw weight is the force in pounds at full draw for recurve archers. Compound archers experience a "peak weight" being the highest force experienced during the draw and a "holding weight," the force experienced at full draw.

EASTON SPORTS DEVELOPMENT FOUNDATION
Established by Jim Easton, ESDF is a non-for-profit foundation that supports the sport of archery by providing grants to programs and organizations throughout the world.

EQUIPMENT SET-UP It is important that equipment is set up correctly to allow the archer to obtain maximum accuracy and performance. Basic variables, once the bow is chosen, are brace height, nocking point location, and centershot (arrow rest position). For the arrows they are: arrow spine (resilience or stiffness), length of shaft, and point weight.

ENDS (IN COMPETITION) Each competition is separated into "ends" which today stands for as number of arrows shot at a target during one segment of the competition (typically 3-6 but can be as low as 1). This term is a carryover from the past in which targets were set up at both ends of the field. After shooting at the targets at one "end" of the field, archers would walk to their targets to determine their scores and retrieve their arrows, then they would shoot back to the other "end" of the field. This practice was abandoned when it was determined to be unfriendly to spectators.

FAST SET GLUE A particular kind of liquid glue that cures almost instantaneously, *e.g.* Superglue, used primarily for attaching fletching to arrow shafts.

FIELD ARCHERY Field archery involves shooting at targets of varying (and often unmarked) distances. Field courses are often set in woodland hills or in the mountains. Typical rounds consist of 14-24 targets, which may have marked or unmarked distances depending on the specific type of round. Archers shoot a small number of arrows at a target and then walk to the target for scoring and then to the next target in sequence.

FINGER TABS Archers use a tab typically made of leather (and metal or plastic) that fits onto the fingers that they pull the bow string with. This provides protection for the fingers from the pressure of the string, helps link the three fingers wrapped around the string together, and provides a slick surface for the string to slide off of.

FITA The International Archery Association, which is an English translation of Fédération Internationale de Tir à l'Arc (FITA), now also called World Archery, regulates and standardizes the rules, policies, and techniques of the archery events of the Olympic Games and other international events involving Olympic-style archery.

FLETCH/FLETCHES/FLETCHING (Feathers, Vanes, Spin Wings) Fletching provides aerodynamic stabilization of arrows with materials such as feathers or plastic vanes attached at the rear of the arrow. Fletching refers collectively to the fins or vanes, each of which individually is known as a fletch. Traditionally, fletching consists of three matched half-feathers attached near the back of the arrow, equally spaced around its circumference. *Spin Wings* is a popular brand of fletch made of Mylar, a modern plastic. Fletches are typically glued on or, in the case of *Spin Wings* attached with double-sided tape. The fletching is used to stabilize the arrow through air resistance in flight. All fletches impart some spin on the arrow and impart a drag on the tail of the projectile to ensure that it does not tumble during flight.

FORGIVING/UNFORGIVING TUNE When an archer has less than a perfect release or weather conditions are less than ideal, a forgiving tune makes it possible to gain a decent score even in the event of a bobble on the part of the archer or inclement weather. An 'unforgiving' tune causes archer's precision to be more important. In windy conditions, an unforgiving tune can cause serious scoring issues.

FRONT OF CENTER BALANCE The point of an arrow must be heavier than any other comparable length of the arrow in order for the arrow's flight to be stable. This means all arrows balance slightly ahead of the center point of the arrow. How far ahead of the center of an arrow the balance point actually is is often stated as a per-cent of the entire length of the arrow. Olympic archers typically have FOCs in the 13-15% range. Most other archers use arrows with lower FOCs.

HOT MELT GLUE A glue that melts when it is heated. "Hot melt" is used to insert arrow points and nock pins into arrow shafts. This is a specially formulated cement, quite different from the hot melt glue sticks available in hobby stores.

HOYT A bow company started by Earl Hoyt in the early 1900's and is an icon in the archery industry.

INDOOR ARCHERY Indoor Archery competitions involve quite short distances from the shooting line to the targets, *e.g.* 18 meters and 25 meters. In a typical Olympic-style round of indoor competition, there are either ten or twenty ends with three arrows each end. Archers have two minutes to shoot each "end" of three arrows.

JOAD The Junior Olympic Archery Development Program is a program of USA Archery to teach archery (recurve and compound) to young people ages 8-20.

JOAD AWARDS Junior Olympic archers can earn achievement awards for shooting both indoors and outdoors with recurve and/or compound bows. The pins are awarded based on achieving specific scores for standard rounds in sanctioned tournaments.

OLYMPIC ACHIEVEMENT AWARD (JOAD) Junior Olympic Archers can earn advanced levels of recognition with the Olympian Award Levels: Bronze, Silver and Gold. These are only awarded for very high performances in sanctioned tournaments.

JOAD AGE GROUPS Competitive groupings are determined by gender and by the ages of the archers: Cubs (12 years old and younger), Cadets (14-17 years old), Juniors (18-20 years old).

LIMBS The upper and lower working parts of the bow, which may be part of a single piece bow or two parts of a three-piece bow (the other part being the "handle" or "riser"). The three-piece bow has the advantage of only needing new limbs for a change in draw weight or a broken limb, instead of a whole new bow.

MARTIN *AURORA* A brand of bow produced by Martin Archery and designed by Mike Gerard and Ed Eliason

NOCKS An arrow nock is the notch attached at the rear of the arrow and is primarily designed to fit around the bowstring and to hold the arrow in place while it is positioned for shooting. Nocks are usually made from plastic and come in a variety of colors.

PIN NOCKS These are nocks designed to fit over a metal insert (a pin) that is glued into the arrow shaft. The pin protects the arrow shaft in the event another arrow hits the nock end of an arrow that is already in the target.

NOCKING POINT To obtain consistent arrow flight, a point on the bowstring must be found at which the force of the string will act directly along the shaft of the arrow. The place on the bowstring where the nock of an arrow is fitted. A nocking point locator is used to make sure this point is used consistently.

NUMBER OF ARROWS SHOT IN TOURNAMENTS There are quite a number of different rounds for both indoor and outdoor archery. Indoor rounds are typically 30 arrows and a double round 60 arrows. Outdoors an Olympic Ranking Round is 72 arrows shot at a 122 cm (48 in) target at 70m distance. A double 70m round is 144 arrows. The FITA International Round is 36 arrows at each distance of 30m, 50m, 70m, and 90m for male JOAD Juniors and men over the age of 20. Females in the same age groupings shoot 36 arrows at each distance of 30m, 50m, 60m, and 70m. Youth distances vary from 15-60m.

OLYMPIC ROUNDS (ORs) or ELIMINATION MATCHES
Olympic Rounds are head to head matches between competitors after being "seeded" in a qualifying round.
Archers who win their matches move on to another
match until the top four archers vie for the Bronze, Silver,
and Gold medals.

OUTDOOR ARCHERY In outdoor competition Olympic
archers shoot from considerable distances (30 meters to
90 meters). Archers compete in all types of weather: rain,
snow, wind, humidity, etc. with the only exception being
when lightning is detected. In the event of a lightning
storm, the tournament is delayed or cancelled. Otherwise,
the archers compete regardless of the weather conditions.

PLUNGER A plunger button is a fine-tuning device consisting of a spring-cushioned tip inside a housing. The
plunger button screws through the riser so that the tip
emerges above the rest. The side of the arrow is in contact
with the tip when the arrow is on the rest. The plunger
button is used to compensate for the arrow's flexing, since
the arrow flexes as the string pushes it with a very high
acceleration.

QUIVER Archers wear a quiver for holding arrows on
their waist/hip while shooting. Typically hip quivers
include tubes to help archers organize their arrows and
keep track of how many they have shot. Pouches are
attached to hold small tools and spare parts.

RECURVE BOW A recurve bow has limb tips that curve
away from the archer when the bow is held. All Olympic
archers use recurve bows. Modern bows incorporate

advanced technologies, like adjustable limb pockets (allowing draw weight and limb angle adjustments), and advanced materials including carbon fiber, forged aluminum, and plastics.

RISER The "handle" of a bow. In a three-piece bow the part to which the limbs are attached.

ROLLING RANKINGS Scores achieved at the events on a 12-month sliding event calendar are used to tabulate Rolling Rankings. Archer's rankings are used to select archers to be sponsored for international competitions.

SCORING In Archery, the targets are marked with ten evenly spaced rings with two consecutive rings sharing the same color. The outer ring is 1 point with each ring adding a point up to the inner Gold which is 10 points. There is innermost ring, half the diameter of the 10-ring, called the X-ring, which is also ten points. The X-ring is used as a tiebreaker in outdoor competitions with whoever scores the greater number of X's wins.

SKI ARCHERY Ski Archery is a combination of Archery and Nordic cross-country skiing and hence is a relative of the most common biathlon (skiing and rifle shooting). It became part of FITA/World Archery in 1991.

SPOTTING SCOPE A telescope that archers use from the shooting line to see their arrow placements in distant targets.

STABILIZERS Weight-bearing rods attached to a bow to balance the bow to the archer's liking, secondarily dampening the effect of torque and vibration produced when shooting.

BOWSTRING The cord that attaches to both limb tips and transforms energy stored in the bent limbs into kinetic energy in the arrow. Modern bowstrings are made a single loops of thread served (wrapped) with additional thread where wear is likely to occur.

TARGET MATT Arrows are shot into matts upon which a target "face" is placed for scoring. Matts are made of twisted grass, compressed straw, plastic foam and other materials.

TARGET ARCHERY Target archery is a popular form of archery in which members shoot at stationary targets at varying distances, usually on a flat field.

USIAC The United States Intercollegiate Archery Championships is hosted by one of U.S. College Archery's member colleges/universities as a four day event. Athletes must meet eligibility requirements, including a 2.0 GPA (3.0 for graduate students), be full-time students at a university/college, and be pursuing a degree.

USCA United States College Archery; a non-profit organization for college archers in all aspects of archery

USA ARCHERY The U.S. Olympic Committee's National Governing Body for target archery in the U.S.

USA ARCHERY RANKING SYSTEM USA Archery has a ranking system for performance at specific national events. The U.S. Archery Team (USAT), established in 1982, consists of the top male and female recurve and compound archers in the country.

V-BARS A part of the most common stabilization system for Olympic bows. The system entails one long rod stabilizer in the front and often two small rods on the sides (the V-bars), which give it a Y shape.

WORLD UNIVERSITY ARCHERY CHAMPIONSHIPS (WUAC) The World University Archery Championships (WUAC) Team Trials are conducted in conjunction with USIAC. WUAC teams are selected based upon the Qualifying portion of the USIAC, which is a double 70 meter round (144 arrows at 70m). The top three in each class (men/women recurve; men/women compound) make up the team.

www.ingramcontent.com/pod-product-compliance
Lightning Source LLC
LaVergne TN
LVHW051519080426
835509LV00017B/2117